Praise

'I have been a Financial Planner for twenty-one years and thought I knew pretty much everything there was to know. However, this book has given me new insights around client needs with regards to trust planning and, more importantly, the personal legacy to family, philanthropy and society at large. I have known Marlene for over twelve years, and she always gives me fascinating opinions on how she sees the world and the financial planning profession. This book is no exception, and I would strongly recommend it to both members of the public and other Financial Planners.'

— **Julian Gilbert**, Director and Certified Financial Planner™, Wealth Matters

'I enjoyed the whole book, but I particularly liked the family and intergenerational aspects. Touching upon charitable giving, faith and the attaching issues was accomplished very well indeed. Faith issues are rarely done, or at least done so well, and this was a standout section for me. Perhaps, as a former Financial Planner, the reason it is rarely addressed so well is why it impacts me among the more "routine issue" chapters.'

— **Lee Robertson**, Co-founder and former CEO of Investment Quorum and co-founder of financial services app, Octo Members Group

'...thorough, thought-provoking and practical. It reads easily and flows well. The book teaches the need for action and is helpful there. I like a prompt! It lived up to my expectations and beyond. A great reference tool.'

— **Stephen A Oliver**, financial adviser and owner of The Will Company

'Too frequently we put off for another day some of the really important decisions that help our children and families make sense of our financial plans when we are no longer able to do so. This lovely book strikes the balance between the practical and the emotional elements of planning. As someone who had to make sense of my father's estate after his death, I cannot imagine how helpful it would have been to have had a book like this – for both of us!'

— **Sir David A Carter**, former National Schools Commissioner and CEO of the Cabot Learning Federation

'I think you have a gem of a book here! This book could be truly transformational to people in later-life planning. I felt excited seeing the content and principles and it was a privilege to read it early – thank you.'

— **Matthew Marais**, Certified Financial Planner and Founding Director of Vertus Capital

'Fail to plan, plan to fail. This book is a clear step-by-step guide to putting your own Family Wealth Plan together, ensuring you have all the tools required to accomplish this and, subsequently, being able to pass your wealth on to those you want to inherit in the most tax-efficient way.'
— **John Luff**, Director of J Wainwright & Co Ltd

'The book is excellent. I have really enjoyed reading it. Many, many readers will say on reading it, "That's me, to a T." This is a book which is relevant to me – and to so many of my 1945 generation.'
— **Gareth Lewis**, formerly the Office of the Independent Adjudicator for Higher Education

MARLENE
OUTRIM

Cascading Your Wealth

How to Build a
Family Wealth Plan
for the
Next Generation

R^ethink

DISCLAIMER

The content of this book is for information only (and pertains only to the law in England and Wales). It does not and is not intended to constitute financial or tax advice. You should undertake your own research and analysis, and take independent advice from a professional before making any decisions or investments, based on your personal circumstances. Neither Rethink Press nor the author can be held liable in respect of any damage, expense, other loss or adverse effects suffered as a consequence of relying on the information provided in this book.

To all my clients who have trusted, believed in and followed my advice to build, protect and cascade their wealth. They have followed the six steps to secure a life well-lived and I have enjoyed their company, their life and family experiences, and 'travelling the world' with them. Without them, I could not have written this book.

Contents

Foreword

My first encounter with Marlene Outrim took place a few years ago, at the Celtic Manor Resort in Newport, South Wales. We gravitated towards each other on the dancefloor, letting off steam after a conference held by the Institute of Financial Planning. I was already aware of Marlene by reputation, through her work as a Financial Planner, and for helping families achieve their wealth ambitions. I just hadn't appreciated her warmth and wit, and her boundless get-up-and-go. As an excellent dancer myself, we hit it off right from the start.

Over time, I would continue to be impressed by Marlene's tireless work ethic and the passion she displayed in her role as a financial planning advocate. When I was forming the Educational Advisory Board for Intelligent Partnership, Marlene was the natural choice to shape our learning and development content for the financial adviser community.

As this book proves, Marlene has a rare gift for grasping technical concepts and for seeing the bigger picture, which she uses for the benefit of her loyal clients. Perhaps due to her time spent as a counsellor, Marlene instinctively knows financial planning goes far deeper than simply knowing how money works. It is just as vital to understand people's motivations and aspirations. If I had to describe Marlene's greatest strength, I would say it is her empathy and way of seeing life through someone else's eyes. Marlene can read people's perceptions (and misconceptions) of wealth, and overcome those invisible psychological barriers that often hold us back from making financial decisions.

When I found out Marlene was writing a book to help families cascade their wealth, I was both delighted and, in many ways, relieved. I knew Marlene was the right person to address this topic, applying the unique combination of head and heart that she has done throughout her career. And, as usual, her timing is impeccable. Family dynamics have shifted dramatically in recent years, but the topic of intergenerational wealth planning hasn't really been fully addressed, until now. While this book has been written for the 'baby boomer' cohort, Marlene takes into account the needs and aspirations of every generation. Her writing is thoughtful, practical and rich with examples from the many clients she has helped down the years.

One area where this book is breaking vital new ground is with the way it addresses financial planning for 'blended' families. The blended family concept has gathered pace in recent years, as more parents have divorced, remarried and brought together children from different relationships. Marlene doesn't shy away from the complexities of modern family life, but addresses them with compassion and understanding, without ever letting emotion cloud judgement.

I am proud to say I'm a member of a 'blended' family myself. My current partner and I both have children from previous relationships, which means that with seven new siblings, my children are part of a much larger family than they were just a few years ago. As well as making Christmas painfully expensive (and more noisy), I now find myself responsible for financial planning decisions that don't just involve me and my partner, but also directly impact family members across three other generations. That's both a privilege and a pressure. I am therefore immensely sympathetic to the growing numbers of my generation who now find themselves in similar situations, with parents, grandparents, children, stepchildren and grandchildren to factor into their financial planning. People simply cannot do it all on their own.

How families pass on their wealth is becoming one of the most important issues of our time, and too many people are still making do without access to quality financial advice. I worry sometimes about the extreme mental stress this can place on those families, especially those that are less confident about making financial decisions.

I consider myself fortunate that the organisation I founded, Intelligent Partnership, is playing a part in helping this overburdened generation, by making sure they have access to the very best standard of financial advice and wealth planning tools as possible. We are giving UK financial advisers, accountants and solicitors the professional resources they need to make sure that every generation, and every corner of society, is supported and cared for. We do this by offering professional learning and development, hosting conferences where Financial Planners can come together and share best practice and create change, and hosting awards that celebrate those exceptional professionals who are making a difference to people's lives.

I know Marlene shares my beliefs about the importance of education, and the need to change people's perceptions of money, which so often begin in early life. Marlene is part of a grass roots movement to encourage better financial education in schools and beyond that leaves people better prepared to face the challenges life will throw at them. At the same time, the younger generation cares more deeply about where money is invested, and believes in the importance of investing sustainably and responsibly. When people turn to financial advisers for help, those advisers need to ensure the advice they give considers their principles as well as their needs. Marlene clearly understands this issue, which will only become more significant in the years to come.

The pandemic has led to more people wanting to do something positive and change their financial situation for the better. What makes this book so important is that it offers those people a way to take care of their own needs, the needs of their family (however extended their family might be) and to also be aware of their responsibility to future generations. But more than anything else, this book is a welcome reminder for all of us that life is there to be lived. Marlene has helped thousands of families to live happier, more rewarding lives down the years. That's an incredible legacy. But knowing Marlene, she is just getting started.

Guy Tolhurst
Managing Director of Intelligent Partnership

Introduction

I have written this book for those who have enough wealth to live comfortably and well. My clients usually have more wealth than they need during their lifetime, and desire to leave a legacy for the next generation, whatever their circumstances. Although there are plenty of guides and tips on how to avoid inheritance tax, it is a complex subject. There is little practical and personal advice about how you can cascade wealth your way and without affecting your lifestyle. You probably also want to live your life well, which means spending money, and most of all, to ensure your own financial security now and in the future. Do you feel reassured your lifestyle will be secure if (say) your partner died, you became disabled or either or both of you required care? This book is for those who want to support the needs of their family alongside their own. Research by Saga Personal Finance shows that many strongly believe it is important to pass on an inheritance to their children and plan to cut back to ensure they have something to pass on.[1]

While you want to cascade wealth to the next generation, you may wish to do this in a way that allows you to retain some control, reduce taxes and without compromising your own lifestyle. This book will help if it is important for you to set up an intergenerational plan for your family. If legacy matters to you and you want it to extend beyond the next generation, or even a multigenerational one, you do not have to be rich to consider these aspects.

It can be difficult to find the right balance, given family relationships, understanding the complexities of inheritance tax, how to use trusts and doing the right thing. Inheritance, taxation, trusts and all their associated rules are complicated.

Sometimes, it is easier to just pass wealth on to your beneficiaries when you die, hoping that they will sort it out amicably between them.

I saw a need for this information to be explained in a manner easily understood and followed. If you follow the six steps as laid down in this book, I can then tailor a plan to suit differing circumstances and needs – the Family Wealth Plan.

I want more people to benefit from my years of experience in helping people achieve the legacy they want, while making the most of their life and their assets.

The plan in this book will help you understand how to navigate your way through the myriad of issues around how to pass on wealth, now and after your death. While you have the time to act, this is your chance to think about what you want to achieve and how best to leave a legacy. Once you have read the book, use the scorecard in the Conclusion to assess your position. You will better understand what actions are necessary and the resources you need, and be confident in carrying those actions out and putting your affairs in order.

Following the six steps in this book, either by yourself or with professional help, will support you to create your own Family Wealth Plan. Think of WEALTH:

1. **W**orking it out

2. **E**valuating

3. **A**nalysis

4. **L**aying the foundations

5. **T**aking action

6. **H**abits for success

These are the six steps to achieving your Family Wealth Plan.

There will be little technical detail or legalese. You can get that from others. This is about the emotional, psychological and practical approaches necessary for the sensitive, but very important, subject of intergenerational wealth.

The Family Wealth Plan

Once you have completed a Family Wealth Plan, you will be free to enjoy the rest of your life, and your money, in whatever way you choose, confident that your wealth will go to the right people or causes. You can put your wealth to good use, without difficulty for family and loved ones.

PART ONE
TAKING STOCK

First things first: what are your objectives in life? It is important to have a view about what will make your life happy and satisfying, and whether you wish to leave a legacy. How do you want to be remembered? You need to know what you own, how much you will need during your lifetime and what a surviving partner or the family will require on your death. Knowing you will have enough money to pay for care costs will help in these decisions. It is worth having some idea what taxes you or your family must pay, during your lifetime but (crucially) on your death. How do you feel about an enormous amount of money being paid to the taxman from your estate? Determining your view on these aspects is paramount before you can even think about cascading your wealth.

ONE
Wealth

Baby boomers currently own over 65% of all UK assets and will need at some stage to transfer this wealth to the next generation.[2] Following the Second World War, a multitude of factors caused the UK birth rate to spike, while the value of assets appreciated more rapidly than they had done in the past. The first decades of the present century have seen property values soar, meaning that many older people have built up considerable wealth in their homes. The result is that the baby boomer generation eventually developed into the largest and wealthiest generational group the UK has ever seen.

HM Revenue & Customs inheritance tax (IHT) receipts show some families are simply not seeking advice for their and future generations' costs, according to Prudential's Wealth Unlocked report of 2021.[3]

And although the pandemic stimulated the need for advice, the number of those adopting wealth transfer strategies remains low.

There may be several reasons for this, which I will explore in this book. One of the main reasons is that people feel concerned about how much they might need for themselves.

Boomers: redefining wealth

Many of you reading this book will have far more wealth than you will need during your lifetime and knowing what to do with this, while alive or after your death, can throw up several issues. There are three obvious places your assets can go when you die: to your family and friends, to charity or to the government as taxes.

When I wrote my book *Boomers: Redefining Retirement*[4] it was about the way the boomer generation – me and my cohort – changed the landscape of retirement, from the traditional 'stop working at State Pension Age', previously 60 and 65. Instead of taking life considerably easier, we want one full of activity, travel and purpose. Many people who retire do not stop working at all but phase into retirement or continue for as long as they can. We still want as much out of life as we ever did, and age will not stop us.

Fortunately, many boomers have known permanent employment, often in the same job for many years, which enabled them to save and invest in property and stocks and shares, while often securing guaranteed and well-paid pensions. More women worked and had full-time careers, a notion that at one time was unacceptable, especially for those who had children. Some of us have inherited from parents, who had bought property themselves, but much of our generation enjoyed a comfortable lifestyle with many of the trappings. Learning from our post-war parents we were still frugal, reduced debt and worked hard.

Other reasons for boomer wealth are that we were the first to benefit from twentieth-century developments such as 'cradle to grave welfare', not to mention free education. Significantly, we have lived through a period of unprecedented economic, social, cultural and technological change. We are the first of these generations to be considered the wealthiest of today's families. However, we are also among the first to experience long retirement along with extended lives. We have needed to be careful and to make sure the money does not run out before we do.

There are estimates that around £5.5trn of intergenerational wealth transfers will occur over the next thirty years.[5] An effective Family Wealth Plan can lessen the likelihood of family conflict, reduce estate costs, reduce taxes and preserve wealth.

Healthier, not just wealthier, lifestyles have become more of a priority for our generation. Despite the effects of ageing, we have still wanted to look and feel good.

Accomplishments and achievements can still be the order of the day but may be more personal: we attain our own objectives rather than those imposed by family or previous employers. They need not be grand or costly, but whatever the activities, they usually lend purpose to our lives. Some of us may take on extra activities, or learning, or just pursue more fully interests we already have. For others, volunteering and contributing to society is a new venture, and a few start a new business.

With time, health and wealth, you have the choice to enjoy life as you see fit, and still take advantage of the opportunities that life offers.

I have advised many clients from this era who, in their 70s and 80s, are getting as much out of life as they can. They are wealthy in relative terms, in that they will not need most of their assets during their lifetimes and inevitably will pass some on to the next generation. How and when they do that is now as much of an issue as making sure their income and investments keep them in the manner they desire throughout their life.

If you are from the baby boom generation and have wealth that you believe will outlast you, it is natural that you should want to help your children and grandchildren (great-grandchildren even) get on the housing ladder or improve their standard of living; but this should not be at the expense of your own financial security in retirement. Financial circumstances can change quickly after death or disability, and it is important that you and your family can contend with events like these. It can mean a careful balancing act to figure out what you can afford to live on and give away. I have had to help families where there has been an unexpected death or sudden long-term illness. Strokes have a way of catching you unaware; your life and that of your family can change within hours.

Almost half of baby boomers say they have so much personal wealth that they can afford to give some of it away during their lifetime. New research shows a similar percentage: 48% of baby boomers say they could afford to give money to family members before they die. Less than a third (29%) ruled this out, and 26% say they are unsure.[6]

While you may not be living in one of the 'hot spots', do not underestimate the wealth you possess. You might see yourself as 'less wealthy' than someone else, but wealth relates to you and how you want to live.

Many people I talk to have not thought about what they want to achieve in the future. Some do not know how much is enough to maintain their lifestyle and those they leave behind. If you have not worked out where you are now financially, and where you want to be, by when and how, you are doing yourself and your family a disservice. Often, this is the first time that partners define and consider the family's vision and mission. The values you hold most dearly will help you clarify these.

Top ten baby boomer hotspots in the UK[7]

Rank	Local authority	County/ region	Total baby boomers	Baby boomers as % of overall population	Average life expectancy at age 65
1	West Somerset	Somerset, South West	11,513	33.39%	21.1
2	North Norfolk	Norfolk, East	32,817	31.34%	21.1
3	East Lindsey	Lincolnshire, East Midlands	43,307	30.98%	19.5
4	Rother	East Sussex, South East	29,239	30.46%	21.0
5	South Hams	Devon, South West	26,055	30.43%	21.2
6	West Dorset	Dorset, South West	31,052	30.22%	20.9
7	West Devon	Devon, South West	16,599	30.04%	20.9
8	Torridge	Devon, South West	20,483	29.83%	20.1
9	Derbyshire Dales	Derbyshire, East Midlands	21,242	29.70%	20.1
10	South Lakeland	Cumbria, North West	30,485	29.45%	21.2

Going back to my Introduction, and regardless of wealth, is an intergenerational plan important to you? Do you want to leave a legacy? You can only really answer these questions once you know whether you have enough for yourself and your family throughout your lifetime.

While I was writing this, *Which?* the consumer magazine suggested that £18,000 a year would cover the 'essential' needs of a couple, and an extra £8,000 annually would help provide for meals out and short-haul European holidays. And if you want health club memberships, long-haul holidays or a new car every five years, then you would need £41,000 a year. *Which?* surveyed nearly 7,000 retirees in February 2021 about their spending, to develop retirement targets for one- and two-person households.[8]

However, according to research carried out by the Pensions Policy Institute (PPI), a think tank, if you want many foreign getaways, home refurbishments and new cars, you will need to save £970,000 in a pension pot.[9] If you are in a couple, you will only need £1.4 million between you, because you will share the costs of living together. This assumes that savers use their pot to buy an annuity (an insurance policy that guarantees an income for life) that increases at 2.9% a year to keep pace with inflation.

A 'comfortable' retirement, according to the Pensions and Lifetime Savings Association, is one during which you can pay for all your basic needs, such as housing costs and bills at £56 a week for food shopping, a three-week holiday in Europe once a year, a second-hand car you replace every five years, and you can afford a new bathroom and kitchen every ten years.[10] Fewer than one in ten people will reach this comfortable standard of living, according to the PPI.

Even among the experts and research there is some divergence on how much is enough. This book will help you determine some of these issues, then help you cascade your wealth in six easy steps.

W is for Working it out

If, during your working life, you have never really had to worry about funding your lifestyle, you just saved for the major things you and maybe your family wanted and there has been more income than you needed, it is probably not until you approach or think about retirement that you wonder whether you have enough. And it is not just money I am talking about, but what you need it for. This is your starting point.

Instead of retirement, I think of financial independence, which is the ability to give up work even if you do not want to. As a baby boomer, you probably still want great fulfilment in life, to be able to maximise happiness when you can, and to enjoy the fruits of your labour. I know I do.

MONEY AND ME

My father was of Chinese extraction but born and brought up in Jamaica. He came to the UK with the *Empire Windrush* and, because of his race, found it difficult to find work. As a result, I come from a very poor working-class background; I can remember my father counting the money every payday to see whether it would pay the following week's bills. Even at that young age, I recall it was a stressful time and, being the eldest, I had to turn away creditors at the door, with the excuse that my parents were out and had not left any money. Debt rolled over week after week, until one day I came home from school to find every stick of furniture gone, taken by the bailiffs. Over the years, my family coped, but never really had much money. Fortunately, I passed the 11 plus, went to grammar school and received an excellent education.

Consciously, I never thought about being rich or having lots of money. Having just enough to pursue the things I wanted in life was sufficient. I had no grandiose or extravagant ideas but just wanted to be like many of my peers, doing a job well, settled into a reasonably comfortable home with a family, and able to pay my way.

My family and friends see me as a generous person because I easily give of what I have, especially money, since I never had it as a child. I do not know what to do with large amounts of money now. I am well-known among friends and family for saying, 'You can have it while I've got it, because when I haven't, you can't.' I realise now that it is because I am uncomfortable with feeling wealthy, so I offload some of it to ease this discomfort. I am not saying that I do not enjoy the finer trappings of life, because I do. I have a lovely home, a great family, many friends, interests, homes abroad and have travelled widely. I know I have enough.

Your story may be quite different, but I am sharing mine with you because it may help you go back to your roots, think about how cash rules and habits in your family have helped you shape your attitude towards money. Understanding the relationship between your finances and what you want out of the rest of your life, what is right for you, is crucial. You need to dwell on this before you can begin to even think about passing on your wealth. Knowing it will help you work out 'how much is enough'.

Think about your goals and values now and what your mission is in life. If you were writing your own obituary now, do you know what you would like it to say?

We are all guilty of not giving enough time to our family and friends, so perhaps this is something you could now address. There are probably activities or interests you have thought about pursuing, but you may not have taken action or found the time. If you can summon up regrets now, what are they likely to be near the end of your life?

Addressing or facing up to some of these questions and issues is the first step in establishing your Family Wealth Plan, then working out whether you have enough to accomplish it. These can be the foundations or the springboard from which you can progress.

Money has many triggers for all of us. It can bring security, safety and pleasure, but it can also bring anxiety and unhappiness. In many families, the subject can be taboo, so these matters are not aired or shared in those families. The riches of a family can also stir up an incredible array of emotions, from greed, grievance, resentment, pain, jealousy and lust, to joy, contentment and satisfaction. This can be because of family culture or traditions handed down, relationships along with emotional taboos. What kind of money traditions and messages have you passed on to your family?

Handing on your wealth may seem an easy exercise to undertake, whether now or later, but understanding your behaviours towards your wealth with its connotations, and sharing this wisdom, may be a more valuable inheritance for the next generation, who you may wish will spend their wealth wisely. Having enough is not about having it all. It is about ensuring that you and your family can get the most out of your lives, have a 'life well-lived', whatever that means to you. Work out what happiness means to you and what you want for yourselves over the next few years, and you can get a handle on how much you might need and whether you will have enough.

While living longer is a blessing, it also brings its problems. Apart from having to strive to be healthier, our money must last longer. Two factors chiefly drive the changing and ageing structure of our population. First, improvements in life expectancy mean that people are living longer and reaching greater ages. Along with this, there has been a decrease in fertility: people are having fewer children and are having children later in life.

I have discussed potential lifetimes with people who have tried to base their longevity on family history. I always challenge this, given that they have and probably still are living a healthier lifestyle than their parents or grandparents. Also, medical breakthroughs mean you are more likely to either recover from, or go on living with, many diseases or illnesses, than to die of them. All this means that you must make sure your money will outlast you and if you want to leave a legacy as well, you need to work out whether you have enough.

Once you have taken this first step – determining your objectives and how you want to live the rest of your life – you can then assess the assets, investments, pensions, protection plans and likely income you will require or be able to build up. There are other issues to consider, such as taxation, inflation and growth. You can work it all out for yourself if you are adept with spreadsheets, but a good Financial Planner will be able to look more dispassionately at you and your circumstances. They will factor in all the various assumptions necessary to make these projections, provide other scenarios and really question how realistic and accurate you are.

But in financial terms, how much is enough?

As part of the planning, my firm gives our clients a full expenditure questionnaire to complete, which may seem daunting, but once done, updating it is easy. This means that we can accurately project how much is enough during their lifetime.

Step 2 of the Family Wealth Plan involves weighing up and assessing how much you have and owe. It means collating information on your assets and liabilities.

E is about Evaluating your assets and liabilities

Once you understand how you want to live the rest of your life, it is important to assess in detail what you own – investments, savings, life policies – and what you owe. I will talk about the family home later in this chapter, and in Chapter Two I will discuss pensions, which can be a complex area. However, having a good understanding of your assets and liabilities will help you evaluate whether you will have enough to fund your lifestyle for the rest of your life.

You may have repaid any mortgage. However, if there are debts, think how these are to be repaid, now or from your estate. A liability may not be a bad thing if it helps to reduce tax, but if interest rates rise, they could eat into your legacy. Not repaying loans while you can afford to may mean a reduction in your standard of living later, or if you need to pay for care.

Checking any life policies to see whether they are still valid and whether they need to be put into trust should also be part of this assessment. As I will show in Chapter Two, doing so may reduce inheritance tax. Do you need more life cover to ensure that on your death, a partner and the family have enough to live on?

Maybe you have some cash savings in the bank or building society, National Savings or Premium Bonds, or in cash individual savings accounts (ISAs). These are 'safe' and secure investments, so it is not surprising that many of you will hold a sizeable amount in cash as security or a 'comfort blanket', even though you might never need to draw on it. The problem with these types of savings is that the interest you receive on them rarely beats inflation, and certainly not at the time of writing. Inflation is the biggest risk to your cash and investments. You can meet your future objectives better by investing.

If the interest you receive is 1% and inflation averages 3%, you are essentially losing 2% of your money every year. Run that forward over a period, and you will see why I feel your 'comfort blanket' should be a small one. Prices, over time, go up and the growth on your investments needs at least to match that, to keep your spending power. Even 0.5% over the average rate of inflation over a few years will help you get to where you want to be; but will that be enough?

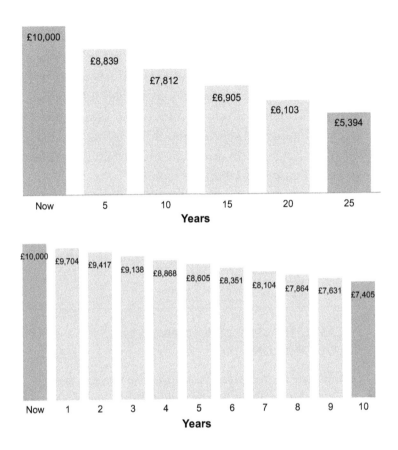

The effect of inflation[11]

The graph above assumes a rate of inflation of 3% each year. That means the purchasing power of £10,000 today could be worth just £4,719 in 25 years. The rate of inflation could actually be higher or lower than 3%.

Of course, inflation affects many investments, not just the money you hold in your bank account.

27

Real growth comes from investing in company shares (equities). Not only can I base this on my experience of investing other people's money for thirty years, but the historical figures we have available. (Of course, past performance is not a guide to the future, but it is a good indicator.) Note, though, investing this way is for the longer term and there are certain principles you must employ to reap the rewards.

There will always be an element of risk in equity-based investments, but carried out well and with advice, ironically they should provide considerable security over the long term.

CASE STUDY: PHILLIP AND INVESTING OVER THE LONG TERM

I met one of my clients, Phillip, over twenty years ago, and he is now about to retire. Until about three years ago (when she died) Phillip lived with his mother; his father died some years previously. Phillip had a steady job and never really spent all he earned. However, he spent most of his spare time caring for his mother, who later became quite immobile. Then she came down with dementia.

When I first met him, he had little capital, but had spare cash he wanted to invest for the long term. We invested it in the Personal Equity Plans (PEPs) that were then available, and in pensions. Every year we met, he would add more money to these, and even in between he would contact me to invest more.

He is currently selling his two-bedroom terraced house to buy a bungalow with land, and looking forward to a

new life. Phillip can do this because, over the years, he
has amassed investments and pensions worth over £1
million. His friends and family would be astonished by
his wealth, but he has achieved this through the sheer
habit of regular saving. He also used me as a sounding
board before major purchases and decisions. It has been
very satisfying to see his life develop in this way.

Foremost, you must decide how much money you
want to keep in cash for emergencies. Set your own
amount, then think about what would help you sleep
well at night. If the amount is large, consider how
much you could put in a fixed-rate bond for a year or
two or in National Savings index-linked bonds.

If you might need cash for other major expenditure,
make sure your plan considers any large purchases,
such as a new car. You can then invest the rest for the
longer term.

There are various ways to invest your money: a stockbroker can advise on individual shares or companies,
and buy and sell the shares for you. A Financial
Planner or adviser usually cannot advise on individual shares; they will direct you to 'pooled' or collective
investments. They may manage their own portfolios
or recommend an external investment manager, or
they may just select portfolios that are ready-made,
such as multiasset multifunds. Usually, this means
that you are pooling your money with other investors
to create a sizeable investment. The fund managers

have the resources and expertise to assess whether a company is worth investing in and will spread their clients' money over a range of company shares or other investments. Financial advisers may advise you to spread your money across several funds.

You can, of course, invest without help; although many think they know how to invest, it is not something I would even consider doing myself. There are too many emotions surrounding the issues of money. There are also cultural and family views that you may not even be aware of that will affect your judgement. This is where a professional can help provide you with the bigger picture and a clearer perspective.

When investing, there are other considerations:

1. Know and understand how much risk you want to take and how you would feel if your investments went down by 50%, as happened in the crash of 2007/8. You do not lose any money unless you sell your investment for less than you paid for it, but nobody really enjoys seeing the value of their funds go down, even if only on paper, and especially if you had not fully understood how you would feel in these circumstances. We call this 'appetite for risk'.

2. Ensure your investment managers spread your investments across different asset classes and geographically ('diversify'). Do not try to guess when the stock markets will rise and fall as

this is just too difficult. With individual shares it may be slightly easier as you trade almost instantaneously, but with collective investment products, often you buy or sell at the next day's price ('forward pricing'), by which time the market can have changed.

The same is true, in spades, of jumping in and out of the market, trying to sell when it is down and then buying back in when the prices have gone up. I know it sounds like common sense, but it is surprising how emotions rule people and drive them to act in ways opposite to their best interest.

3. Be as tax-efficient as you can, using tax wrappers such as ISAs each year.

It will cost you to invest. While you probably do not think there are any costs associated with cash savings, the interest rates the banks pay you for using your money are considerably lower than what they charge the borrowers that they lend your money to. The difference is the cost that you are meeting, though you might not realise this. All investments have a cost over and above the price of the stocks or shares; fund managers charge a range of fees, stockbrokers charge trading fees, you may have to pay stamp duty, and custodians charge for looking after your investments (you will probably use a custodian though it might be hidden within an overall service, such as a stockbroker's account). When you receive advice, that carries a charge, too. If you can make a good return, you will more than cover these costs and will see them as worthwhile. Passing on wealth to the next generation means you need long-term growth.

Do not forget any inheritances you believe you are likely to receive and whether you will need them in order to realise any part of your plan.

Next, we consider another type of investment: that most special asset, the family home.

The family home

Consideration of the home and its value is an important aspect in working out what you own. There is every possibility that your home may be the biggest part of your wealth, although this is not always the case. It is also possible that some of your estate includes a property portfolio, although for this book, I will focus mainly on your principal residence.

It is interesting to bear in mind that the principal residence can provide options for cascading your wealth, but remember: while it is an important asset, it is your home.

I have spoken to many retirees who are keen to stay in the family home, regardless of size and upkeep. They have probably spent thousands of pounds getting it just how they want it and they enjoy their surroundings and the familiarity. They can usually afford the upkeep and to pay for someone to help care for it. Even when bereaved, they might continue living there. One client inherited the family home, a Grade One-listed building with twenty-nine rooms. Yet despite being single and now retired, she intends to remain there for as long as she can, as her widowed mother did before her.

Then there are those who, because of failing health and mobility or fear of it, just want to downsize to something more manageable. Often people may just want to improve their home and make it more comfortable. Indeed, a few will buy a better house or move to a better area when they retire, or just nearer to family.

Whatever your views about your home, it will figure significantly in your Family Wealth Plan and the plan for passing on your wealth. I will go into more detail in the inheritance tax section of Chapter Two about leaving your home to your heirs.

How you and your partner each write your wills and how you own the property, jointly or as tenant in common, is important. If owned jointly, on death, the house will automatically pass to the surviving partner, as will the reliefs on inheritance tax, with no tax to pay. However, if you own it as tenants in common, strictly you each own half of the house. This means that you could leave your share of the property to someone other than your partner.

The only problem with this is that you might wish to be sure that your partner would have sufficient to live on after you die. While you might make them a life tenant, so they could remain in the property for the rest of their life, the person or persons who owned the other half could force a sale. You might have written your will well enough to prevent this, and a letter of wishes would do much to bind the decision (see Chapter Six). But imagine this occurring when you are elderly, possibly frail. While you might be confident that your children would never oust you from your home, their partner might convince them that this would be the right action. Or imagine that you divorce your partner: this could mean that part of the property counts in the financial settlement, and would force a sale with you being compelled to find other accommodation, much against your wishes.

Leaving the house to the next generation on death is one consideration, but you may have other reasons for wanting to sign over the house now. This is a perfectly good option, but there are costs and downfalls for this. You could lose another allowance called the residence nil-rate band (RNRB) which you can offset against the family home if you do not take proper advice. Moreover, if you give away your home, you cannot derive any benefit from it. So, if you sign over your home to your children but continue to live in it, this can count as a 'gift with reservation' and the value count for inheritance tax (see Chapter Five). The only way around this would be to pay a market rent to your children. You could reduce this by whatever you spend on the property's maintenance. Few people with whom I have discussed this like this idea. Records and an audit trail would be necessary as evidence that you have kept to the rules.

The same applies to holiday properties once the parents realise they must pay a market rent to stay there for any period. Short social stays can occur. Your children would have to pay income tax on any rent that you pay to them and capital gains tax when they sell the house.

Likewise, if you pass investment properties directly to your children or to a trust, this will trigger capital gains tax and you may not continue to receive rental income from them.

The government website states that Stamp Duty Land Tax (SDLT) may need to be paid if the 'ownership of land or property transfer[s] to you in exchange for any payment or "consideration"'. The circumstances of a transfer can affect which rules apply. If you give a majority share of the property to a person who makes no payments in return, then no exchange of money is given, even where you take on liability for a mortgage. This is the case even if the share you retain is worth more than the SDLT threshold. But if you take over some or all of an existing mortgage, you will pay SDLT if the value of the mortgage is above the SDLT threshold. Some people may leave part of their estate, such as their property or land, to a person in their will. 'If you get land or property under the terms of a will, there is no need to tell HMRC and you will not pay SDLT', Gov.uk states.[12]

This is another complex area on which you should seek advice, especially if you are looking to transfer property into a company. You can use hold-over relief to defer any gains until the new owner sells. You can claim this through HMRC but again you should consult a professional in this area.

If you die within seven years after any land or property is transferred, it becomes a 'potentially exempt transfer' (PET) and HMRC will tax part, or all, of the value.

Finally, if you transfer the family home and later need local authority care, the authority might claim that you had intentionally 'deprived' yourself of assets.

So, although there are several options available if you wish to share the ownership of your home, you need to have thought through your motivation, what the outcome would be and whether it would achieve the objective you desire. Most important of all, remember that, by giving away the home, you cease to be the legal owner and the new owners can do what they like with what is probably one of your proudest and most valuable possessions. There are other options to outright gifting of the home to your children, which I will address in Chapters Two and Six.

Summary

Having a clear understanding of how you want to live the rest of your life, and what you want to achieve, is the first step in the WEALTH process. Make sure you discuss these with your partner to assess how closely aligned your objectives are. There is no point following one route only to discover that they had another idea altogether.

Step 2 is appraising your assets and liabilities, their values, your income and the cost of your lifestyle as the next stage to constructing your Family Wealth Plan. Recognising that this is just not about the financial state of your affairs, but also an emotional appraisal is an important first step in the journey you are about to take. You can adapt and amend this blueprint as circumstances change. It will take time to develop a Plan, but it will take less time to make any changes along the way, if you need to take a different path.

TWO
A Is The Analysis

As part of the next stage, working it all out, there are issues to be thrown into the mix which will need some discussion, to assess how you feel about them before you can properly define your plan. Once you have Worked out your life goals and Evaluated what you own and owe, these data go alongside the Analysis you now must carry out. With this stage, number three, you may need the help of an expert, not only to ensure you have all the information needed, but to help you make sense of it all. A third party will be more objective and consider your plan as a whole, and whether there are any problems with it.

You may have already thought about how you would deal with the matters that this chapter covers. However, other options that I want you to consider may affect how you decide to proceed, ultimately. Further research may be needed before final analysis can take place. It is time to work everything out and factor in these crucial aspects.

Inheritance tax

If you are serious about passing on part of your wealth to the next generation, then you must consider any potential IHT. By doing so, you can ensure that you give the maximum possible as a legacy to your family, friends and loved ones and not too much, if anything, to the taxman, since you can avoid doing so.

Your views on this tax are important as any adviser would want to know whether this is an area of work they must consider. HMRC provides many ways to mitigate the tax, so we can only find approaches that suit your circumstances if we fully understand how far (if at all) you want to take advantage of these. If you do not wish to do anything at all about IHT, we need to know that. People's opinions vary widely.

According to Consumer Intelligence a third of consumers aged 55 and over who take financial advice have not yet considered IHT planning.[13] You do not have to be rich to fall into the IHT bracket: the average price of property on its own can mean you catch the taxman's attention.

Inheritance tax: analysis of receipts (£ million)[14]

Year of death	2010-11	2011-12	2012-13	2013-14	2014-15	2015-16	2016-17	2017-18	2018-19	2019-20
Transfers taxable at death	2,631	2,828	2,955	3,303	3,659	4,449	4,647	5,004	5,081	4,814
Transfers to discretionary trusts	11	12	9	20	13	14	18	21	22	26
Charges on discretionary trusts	76	62	141	80	132	187	159	180	255	282
Net cash receipts	2,718	2,903	3,105	3,402	3,804	4,650	4,824	5,205	5,359	5,122
Additional non-cash	6	15	42	15	22	24	16	13	25	40
Total receipts	2,724	2,917	3,147	3,417	3,825	4,673	4,840	5,218	5,384	5,161

Note: 2019–20 figures are provisional; 'trust' figures include other relevant property trusts

Inheritance tax facts and figures from HMRC

In 2017–18, 3.9% of UK deaths resulted in an IHT charge, 0.7% fewer than in 2016–17. This year was an exception: since 2009–10 the percentage has steadily increased. The fall is likely due to the introduction of the residence nil-rate band (RNRB) tax-free threshold in April 2017.

However, in 2021 the Chancellor froze IHT allowances for the next five years, which means that more people are likely to become liable for inheritance tax, especially if house and stock market prices continue to rise.

Prudential recently carried out a survey asking why so many families leave in-life wealth transfer so late. They commissioned research with over 1,000 adults who had employed a financial adviser in the previous five years, with interviewees drawn from all 'decision-making' generations.[15] Their findings include the following:

1. The most common reason was 'I might need it myself in the future', felt by 29% of those interviewed. Understandable, perhaps, given increasing life expectancy and the cost of care.

2. 'Squandering' was second (25%), a concern that generations to come might fritter away the older generation's hard-earned savings.

3. 'A lack of control over their spending' (22%), which echoes 'squandering'; older generations are looking for ways to direct how younger generations put assets to constructive use.

4. 'They should make their own way in the world'. A high one in five participants (rising to 29% of grandparents) believe independence is an important life lesson, at least in the early years.

5. Of the sample, 19% were concerned 'Recipients would need to pay tax' on any gifts.

Who must pay inheritance tax?

Many people view IHT as a stealth tax, as they do not realise that the estate must pay this on death and that it is calculated on all your assets, except for most pensions. There is no tax to pay between husband and wife, or civil partner (but IHT becomes payable on the second death for such couples). You would have checked out the value of your home and other assets in the Evaluation step (see Chapter One), but the values calculated on your demise may be far higher than you or your family ever expected. Accordingly, review your figures regularly so there will be no shocks and you can plan for any eventualities.

The tax is currently 40% of your total estate above:

- £325,000 per person – the nil-rate band (NRB) – plus, if you have children and you have left your principal residence to them in your will

- £175,000 per person – the residence nil-rate band (RNRB)

Every individual has a nil-rate band and married couples and registered civil partners can pass this to the surviving spouse/partner, so that on the second death the NRB is £650,000 (or £1 million if RNRB applies), so long as you (or your spouse) have not transferred or given any of your estate to anyone else in the meantime.

Your executors must work out and pay the tax from your estate, normally within six months of your death. Late payments attract a levy.

NRB planning used to be popular: couples used to change the ownership of properties from 'joint' to 'tenancy in common' so that in their wills they could gift half of the home (and/or their estate up to this amount) on the death of the first partner. On the second death, another IHT allowance could be used. On the face of it, this was sound advice but sometimes we have short memories, time passes and we may forget about the emotional and practical implications of giving away half of the house; until one of you dies and discussion takes place about the ownership of the home.

How is the tax calculated?

- Work out the value of the assets in your estate.

- Clarify how the assets are owned.

- Calculate the total value of the assets in each part of the estate.

- Deduct the value of any debts and liabilities that need to be paid out of the estate.

- Determine the amount of any IHT relief and exemptions (including, but not limited to, the NRB and/or RNRB).

- Check the amount of any recent charitable donations.

- Consider the current value of the NRB.[16]

- Add the value of gifts the deceased made in the seven years before death.

There is a useful IHT calculator on the Gov.uk website.

These tips may help you make some calculations yourself, but experts might point out matters you may not have considered that can affect the final amount of IHT.

Add to this the fact that the rules of inheritance tax are complex. In reviewing any lifetime gifts you must distinguish between 'chargeable transfers (CTs)' and 'potentially exempt transfers (PETs)'. These are treated differently in working out IHT. The timing of them is crucial and you must meet various conditions for them to work.

In addition, your estate must pay any tax owed before probate can be granted, ie before it gains access to any of the estate and the ability to pay that tax. There have been some minor changes – an executor can now arrange for some or all the tax to be paid directly from savings or investment funds in your estate – but if much of the value is a property, that may need to be sold in order to pay the tax and get probate.

To avoid this, a loan may be necessary to pay the tax, or the executors can ask to be allowed to pay in instalments over ten years. This can be quite a heavy liability as the Capital Taxes Office (CTO) imposes interest rates which are significantly higher than current rates.

CASE STUDY: ELLEN

An unmarried client faced a large tax bill when she inherited the family home and other property. Ellen's mother, who had died suddenly, had left the investments and cash to her married sons, who had children. Ellen had little in savings to pay the bill immediately, so applied for six-year repayment. It proved to be a heavy burden each year: the CTO added 10% interest. Once probate was granted, she was able to release equity from one property to pay the balance, which proved less expensive. Ellen was greatly relieved.

There have been proposals to simplify the rules on IHT, but I doubt that will happen soon, given the current Conservative government's full agenda with the effects of the coronavirus pandemic, Brexit and the need to find funds to cover the cost of aiding businesses during this time. As already mentioned, the Chancellor Rishi Sunak froze the nil-rate band and the residence nil-rate bands for five years from April 2021. This was to assist the growth in the economy following the debt gained and the money provided during the pandemic crisis.

However, there is still scope to work within the current rules, provided you understand them or get guidance through them. There are many exemptions, allowances and reliefs that you can take advantage of, and I will provide more detail on these in Chapter Five.

Some people say that IHT is a voluntary tax. If you have now worked out what your potential bill might be, do you want to use this opportunity to save your family from paying too much tax, or any at all? Developing your Family Wealth Plan will help you achieve this, perhaps altogether, maybe in part. It will help you decide how much you want to give to your family or partner, now or after your death. It will show whether you will be able to maintain the lifestyle you desire, no matter what happens. You will not have to fear running out of money if you give some away.

Costs of care

Whatever the state of your health now, one issue that may prevent you from passing on your wealth is any long-term illness requiring professional care, whether at home or in a residential facility. With people living longer, inevitably the effects of ageing, any underlying conditions and just not living healthily enough will catch up with you. Stroke or dementia are other illnesses that may catch you or your loved ones unaware. These might be supportable in your home in the early years, but eventually will require some outside support. Clients have often said to me they were afraid to spend their money for these very reasons and they wanted to ensure that they and/or a partner could afford the best care available.

Early on, if you need help, then paying for a cleaner, a home carer for a few hours or for meals to be delivered may not prove too expensive. Attendance Allowance, which is not huge but is tax free, may help. Overnight stays, help with mobility and personal cleanliness and possibly respite care can prove to be more expensive. The fees for residential care in a reasonable home can vary depending on where you live, the facilities required and what is available. In England, for example, care homes in London are more expensive than care homes in the north-west or south-west. Find out how much care home fees are near you.

In a care home, nursing care is more expensive than residential care. Care homes that provide specialist care, for conditions such as dementia, will normally charge a higher fee. Dementia care needs specialist aid and beds may not be readily available in your area. This means making many enquiries and you may have to pay more, to get what you want at a convenient location. Being aware of prices and how much you can expect to pay will help you make important decisions about your own or a loved one's care.

According to carehome.co.uk,[17] in 2021 the average weekly cost of living in a residential care home was £704, while the average weekly cost of a nursing home was £888 across the UK. The monthly average cost of residential care was £2,816 and receiving nursing care in a care home cost on average £3,552 per month.

Far fewer people than ever before are now eligible for state funding for elderly care, so most times you may need to fund at least an element of care privately. If required, care costs (of whatever type) will add up.

Only 27% of the population have planned how they would fund potential care, yet 75% of people are likely to need care at some point.[18]

If care can be provided at your home, family members may be available to provide support, and reduce costs. For instance, if family members can help one week out of four, that cuts the cost by a quarter; help at weekends may have a similar effect (because professional care costs more at weekends). This sort of flexibility is simply not possible in a care home.

Care homes present their own issues, since empty beds mean lack of income and there can be staff problems, so the best homes are likely neither to be cheap nor to often have vacancies.

It is not surprising, then, that finding and paying for care can be a big worry for many retirees and that there may be a reluctance to part with any capital that they do not need at the moment. If you are reading this book, reassurance on this possible heavy expense is paramount. Often, it is your partner who gives the most support if you need help day to day, so it is essential that they get all the practical and emotional support they need. If you contact your local authority and ask them to assess your care needs, they can look at support for your partner at the same time, with a carer's assessment. Most local authorities offer a range of services to support carers, such as temporary care for you to give your partner some time out for themselves, or details of local carers' support groups and services to lend a little help around the home.

If you have a serious physical or mental health condition and you need ongoing care, the NHS may provide it free. NHS continuing healthcare can include a place in a care home, or a care package to help you continue living in your home. Even if you are not eligible for

NHS continuing healthcare, you might still get some help with your nursing care, free, though applying for this can be extremely difficult.

You may have thought about trying to avoid paying such high fees and there are a few ways to achieve this, which I will not go into here. The local authority can take action to prove 'deprivation of assets' and possibly come after you or the person to whom you gave assets. Alternatively, they can include your property when they calculate the value of your assets, which is part of the assessment for local authority support; or means-test you, using their assessments of the values of the funds available to you – so you will gain nothing from attempting to hide assets.

You cannot simply give your money away, although sometimes doing so is perfectly legitimate and this book will show you how. There are sound reasons you can put forward if you wish to give away your assets without them potentially being taken into account for calculating care fees.

Equity release or home reversion plans can also be used to help fund care.

Are you in denial as your health deteriorates? Even though you approach old age with mobility issues or memory loss, do not delay considering residential care. If you do not open yourself to this possibility, you may fail to make any financial provision for care.

Taking this decision at the right time can significantly increase the likelihood of you being able to keep your property, leave an inheritance and retain some disposable income.

CASE STUDY: OPTING FOR CARE

Robert's wife, Esther, had dementia and needed to go into care. Robert was of sound mind and in a reasonable physical state. He had always looked after the finances. Their estate amounted to over £1 million, including the value of the house. However, he did not wish to live alone and opted to go into care at the same time. He wanted to hand over responsibility for their money and assets to an attorney. This may have seemed unusual to some, but Robert had very definite ideas about how he wanted to live the rest of his life. Robert and Esther were in their late 80s.

Things to consider

Your funds and assets: How much money do you have and how much do you need? We examined this in Chapter One.

Benefits and pensions: Are you claiming all you are entitled to? For example, women and men whose spouse or civil partner died before 2005 in the armed services may also claim an additional bereavement allowance or war widower's pension.[19]

Your prognosis: Is your health likely to stay the same or deteriorate? Have you budgeted for either eventuality?

Inheritance plans: Do you wish to pass on some of your wealth to your family and is IHT an issue for you?

There are many options for paying for care, such as:

- Lifetime annuity
- Rental of property rather than selling it
- Deferred payment schemes, although these are limited
- Using your savings, investments and pension
- Equity release

The key to providing for care home fees is to plan *as early as possible.* Look at where you are now, work out where you want to be and what you want to achieve, and make all of this part of your Family Wealth Plan.

Pensions and planning

Having a better understanding of any pension funds you have and how they can help you cascade your wealth is another part of the equation. There is more to pensions as part of your planning than just a set of figures. Here, I am talking about pension funds or pots and pensions in payment. If you are one of those fortunate enough to have a generous pension from an employer, with guarantees to boot, you are probably enjoying the income from that right now.

Final Salary or Defined Benefit Schemes have become increasing costly for the employer, partly due to people living longer, so many have closed, some folded, others been transferred to another regime. These days they are few. Some of these have stopped new members from joining, to limit their liabilities, and the sponsoring employer has started a new plan without the same guarantees, for example a Defined Contribution or 'Money Purchase' Scheme. These have no guarantees but rely purely on the contributions made and investment growth.

Pensions are now a difficult area for planning, and I do not want to get into too much detail for fear of turning you off. They are, however, an essential part of building a picture of where you are now. They now provide greater flexibility and accessibility than they used to, which means they can be a valuable tool for cascading your wealth. In the past, you used a pension pot to buy an annuity to fix an income for life, after possibly taking a tax-free lump sum. You could include certain guarantees, a spouse's pension when you died and regular increases each year. (All these add-ons reduced the starting payment.) But the payment was for life and if longevity was part of your genetic make-up, then they could be good value for money. There are insurers who offer special rates for people who smoke, or with certain health conditions. Now that has all changed: people with a 'Money Purchase' Pension Fund can draw on it, as and when they wish, much like a bank account, although you must pay income tax on 75% of that fund.

Pensions rarely attract IHT, and while some schemes (often, older insurance policies or Defined Benefit Schemes) only allow you to leave your pension to a spouse and/or dependants still in full-time education up to the age of 21, others allow you to leave pension pots to anyone: charities or your best friend if it suits you. You will need to consult the rules of the scheme. Almost all schemes ask you to complete a 'nominated beneficiary' form, naming those to whom you wish the scheme trustees (or manager) to give your benefits when you die.

A pension is only taxable once you start to draw it. If you die before the age of 75 there is no tax to pay, but after that your beneficiaries pay income tax at their marginal rate. They can draw your remaining fund down in tranches, and with some suitable advice they could keep taxation to a minimum.

You can leave pension pots to beneficiaries, who will incur no IHT liabilities provided that when you retired your pot was worth less than a Lifetime Allowance (currently £1,073,000),[20] although there may be income tax considerations. It might make sense for some of you to use the money tied up in your property before accessing pension assets, especially with average equity release rates currently sitting at 2.8% fixed for life. Since pensions were relaxed, more people tend to consider how equity release can be useful within broader estate planning. It is not a simple area of financial advice, and the approach taken depends on family circumstances and individual preferences. While payments from most pension funds are exempt from IHT, not all of them are.

If transferring a Final Salary or a Defined Benefit Pension to a Money Purchase Scheme or a Personal Pension Plan, take care: if you were in poor health at the time of transfer and you die within two years, HMRC may view this as a tax avoidance tactic. In *HMRC v Parry & others* [2020] UKSC 35 the deceased had transferred her pension shortly before she died and not yet drawn her pension so that death benefits became payable to her sons. The court decided that the failure to exercise the right to take a lifetime pension should be treated as a disposition made immediately before her death. Although the woman concerned died in December 2006, well before the pension changes described above, the case has some useful guidance.

If you or your named beneficiaries do not need to draw income from a pension, you can cascade it down through the generations. It can, therefore, be a valuable planning tool. Calculating and working out whether any of this part of your wealth is necessary to maintain your lifestyle for the rest of your life is part of producing the Family Wealth Plan. Other than naming your beneficiaries, there are no special steps to be taken, other than making sure to invest it wisely. If at some stage you find you need some of your pension money, then you can access it and leave the rest to those of your choice.

Using a 'spousal bypass' trust gives greater control over pension funds. Although someone who receives your pension fund after your death may take your wishes into account, they do not have to, and might pass this on to their own children or those of the new partner on divorce and remarriage (see Chapter Three on 'blended' families). A spousal bypass trust means that on your death the pension funds go into the trust, and you can nominate how you wish the trustees to distribute them.

CASE STUDY: DANIEL PASSING ON WEALTH IN HIS LIFETIME

Daniel, who is single, with no children or dependants, has always worked in the City of London and at age 76, he still does. He has always earned a high salary with bonuses, and has accumulated a fair amount of wealth, as well as pensions worth over £800,000 more than the Lifetime Allowance. If he drew this pension, he would pay a penal rate of tax on it.

He can afford to retire and lives on his savings and investments, so any pension benefits are superfluous to his needs. His beneficiaries will have to pay a hefty sum in IHT when he dies; but he could draw 25% tax free from his pension as a lump sum and give this to his only relatives while still alive. They will inherit the rest, free of IHT, but will pay income tax at their highest rate on it; or draw it down in tranches when their tax rate is lower, say after they retire. They can pass it on to the next generation or give it to charity. The money can cascade down through the generations.

While living off his other assets, Daniel hopes he can reduce his estate by the time he dies and thereby some of the tax bill.

This is not a typical case, but Daniel's concern is that both he and his relatives might lose the pension benefits he had built up over the years if he does not take this action.

Unscrupulous advisers can easily convince those with guaranteed pension schemes to transfer them into personal pensions, to access them this way. Being able to leave these funds to the next generation is attractive. However, on transfer they lose potentially valuable guarantees (such as a pension for a surviving spouse if the pension-holder should die first).

It is easy to get carried away by the large cash values that pensions can represent, especially if the employer is keen to reduce the liability to pay this income from its fund. For some it may be a good move to transfer out, but unless they take sound advice, they could not be sure. Many who did not, have been open to exploitation and lost their whole pension.

So, while on one hand the choices now available can facilitate creative planning and ensure security for you and your family, on the other you could be in danger of making some major losses, without proper advice.

Another warning: pension rules could change in the future. If pensions are a major part of your overall wealth, understanding the role they will play should be an important consideration.

Seven ways to mitigate inheritance tax

To assist you with your thinking how best to proceed, I will now examine how you can legitimately avoid your descendants having to pay IHT, but all require some planning. The earlier you can start this, the better and the less costly it will be for you and your beneficiaries. I have spoken to enough families to know that it is painful.

Here, I will mention seven different ways, but I will describe each in more detail later in the book. It is important for now that you consider whether any of them are suitable options.

I always ask my clients how they feel about any tax being paid on their deaths. It is such a personal question that answers can range from not wanting a penny to go to the taxman to the view that the inheritance will more than cover any costs. There is no correct answer, but you need to be honest about how you feel about this subject. Your view should determine which options you prefer.

1. Your first choice would be to spend all your money before you die. Of course, that would be more straightforward and easier to accomplish if you knew how long you were going to live; then you could work out how much you need each year to maintain your lifestyle, allow for some major expenditure, then divide by the number of years you think you will live. Of course, life is not that simple, and there are always uncertainties that could use up your money before you are ready.

   This might make you feel insecure and keep more capital for your needs than you require during your lifetime, but it gives a margin of comfort.

2. Second, you could give your money away. Here lies a similar danger: if you give money directly to a person, could you ever ask for it back if you needed to? Placing assets in a trust where you can protect them until the beneficiaries can access them is another option, but in the past trusts in less than expert hands, or trustees receiving bad

advice, have had bad press. Also, there are many types of trust, so ensuring you have the right one for you and your beneficiaries is not a simple matter.

In some circumstances, gifting into trust requires you to survive the gift by seven years, and time may not be on your side.

You could also make donations to recognised charities, national museums, universities, political parties and some other institutions.

3. Third, you could put existing life policies into trust to avoid the benefit forming part of your estate. Of course, this depends on the type of life policy you have, and what trust you use. This is a simple and inexpensive way of saving tax.

   You can also set up a life insurance policy purely to mitigate any tax bill. This is something that you can do relatively easily. While it will not reduce the IHT that will ultimately be payable, the sum insured can be paid tax free to those you nominate without having to wait for grant of probate. This can act as a core for a wider approach, which you can vary within certain limits over the years.

4. As well as leaving your pension pot for your family, you can fund a pension for another person, and this need not require huge layout provided you start early enough. There are some exceptions, though.

5. Normal gifts out of income are often overlooked. You should by now have established whether your income regularly exceeds your expenditure. If you do not spend the excess, but save or invest it, then this will add to the ultimate IHT bill. Making gifts out of this income prevents that and, given in the right way, can mitigate tax.

6. You can apply for equity release, to raise capital to cover gifts to your family or personal spending, and to safeguard your pension pot (in the main, this does not attract IHT). By accessing cash from your property to live on, you avoid drawing on the pension. You can pass this on with little risk of IHT liability.

   Equity release is a debt on the estate on your death, reducing IHT. However, it is vital that people get specialist advice before making any choices around IHT or how to use any housing equity.

7. Business property relief (or BR as it is more commonly known) was introduced in 1976 to allow family businesses to be passed down through generations, free of IHT. However, the rules enable smaller investors to benefit, without owning a business. BR mitigates IHT if you invest in shares of a company which has been trading for two years. If you have left planning late, then this can be a good option. In fact, if your ISA holdings have grown over the years, it might be worth switching some of these to BR investments. You might

consider Alternative Investment Market (AIM), impact or ethical investing at the same time. This is a quick and easy way of mitigating IHT.

You save 40% tax for your family with any of these choices. Clearly, not all will be suitable, but a mixture may bring you the best result. Analysing all the choices and working out what suit your circumstances best is the most important stage after you have worked out what you have, what you need and what you can and want to give away, either now or later. Making use of the various exemptions which are available and funded regularly means you can legitimately avoid a sizeable amount of IHT over time with small amounts of outlay.

I have great discussions with my clients around these choices. Once someone has prepared a Family Wealth Plan we can go through a process of elimination, weighing up the pros and cons of each approach. It can be a slow process, which is why it is good to start sooner rather than later.

Alongside this will be the time you wish to devote to estate planning, what knowledge and experience you have, how much risk you can tolerate. There is no 'one size fits all' approach.

Summary

By now you will have worked through steps one to three of your Family Wealth Plan. The most important elements are your objectives and what it is you want to accomplish.

Add to these elements how far you wish to mitigate tax, and whether you want to make gifts, when and how. Is the transfer of part or all of the family home an important part of your plan? What should happen to your pension funds and who should benefit from them if you do not use all the funds?

Step 4, Laying the foundations, starts making sense of all of this and reflecting it in your plan. Cashflow modelling will be a necessary ingredient in calculating whether every part is achievable. The result is your Family Wealth Plan, which will help you cascade your wealth in a way that suits you. It will accommodate your beneficiaries' needs and keep you in the manner to which you have become accustomed. So, it matters that you take stock, work it all out and be clear about the choices you make. However, laying the foundations is not easy, as Chapter Three will show: others and their lifestyles may impinge on you and yours, and the decisions you make. Working through these will make the last two steps much easier.

PART TWO
A FAMILY AFFAIR

In life and death, you are a member of a family. Married, single, with or without children, you are a member of a family. And nowadays four generations could be alive at the same time. Intergenerational wealth is a growing issue, yet it seems to be rarely discussed within families. What happens in your family? There may be some difficulties to face with them, yet there are also a range of openings for connecting and communicating.

THREE

Challenges And Obstacles

Whatever type of family you are from, relationships are rarely plain sailing throughout your life. Even if you are fortunate enough to experience few disputes or upheavals, circumstances beyond your control can force disagreements, stressful situations or complications. By gaining some insight into potential problems, and expecting them, you can sometimes find solutions. To develop a successful Family Wealth Plan, consider what problems there may be in your family. Here are some pointers.

Blended families

Whether because of divorce or death, there are now many 'blended families' in the UK. A blended family comprises a couple, their children from previous relationships and the children they have had together. The current Prime Minister Boris Johnson and his wife Carrie Symonds are very much part of a blended family arrangement with their son, Wilfred, having at least five half-brothers and -sisters making up his family unit.

Families in modern society, whatever structure they take, often face financial problems and want the opportunity to look after themselves within their own family unit rather than look to the government for help.

Besides the growing number, the nature of blended families continues to become more complex. Research by Ortiz-Ospina and Roser found that four out of every ten British marriages end before their twentieth anniversary.[21] This is mainly through divorce, but sometimes through bereavement. Of those whose marriages end, half will marry again. The result of all of this is an ever-growing number of blended families. While these types of family may appear challenging at first, they come with a great opportunity to build estate plans that work in the best interests of every family member.

It is not always easy to divide your wealth, even if you have been in a relationship for many years and all your children were born within that relationship. Imagine how complicated it can be if you divorce, legally separate, then have children with a new partner. If you have been through this experience, you know that getting divorced or separated is a stressful and painful process, especially when the two of you sort out finances and assets. The financial implications of a second divorce are likely to be severe and need to be considered by both parties. Circumstances around a second marriage are almost always more complicated.

You may have considered a pre-nuptial contract before remarrying. This sets out what a couple would like to happen to their possessions should the marriage break down. The subject of inheritance can be a complicated one that needs to be considered when embarking on a second marriage. Your new partner could easily have a family of his or her own. You may trust that, if you should die before your new partner, they will pass on your share of the estate to their stepchildren, but circumstances can change. The surviving partner may meet someone else and may have more children with them. It does not always follow that the partner will follow your wishes, leaving their estate to their children or family and dealing with yours as you intended.

There can be conflict (in your own mind or between you and your partner) between wanting to ensure that you provide well for your partner and leaving an inheritance for your children. By the time of your death, your children may be adults, perhaps with children of their own and expecting an inheritance. You may or may not have discussed this with them. They may have built up hopes and anticipation, only to have them dashed and you unable to help them.

Relationships between family members will feature strongly in all this. They may have complications, even if on the surface everyone seems to get along. There is nothing like money to show any cracks or different agendas. Also, the circumstances of different family members may influence any decisions. While some may be successful and financially well off, others may be in poorer straits. Who should deserve more?

It is therefore crucial that you each make a will and seek professional advice if you cannot agree on how to divide up your estate on death. It may be sensible to choose a will writer who will do free rewrites or codicils (for example, the Will Company offered this at time of writing). The will you write now may change later.

If the two of you are not married, then it is equally important to write a will that is clear about the different relationships in your family, identifying stepchildren and children. If the will writer assumes your partner's children are yours, it can cause complications. This is an area where you need to be quite specific, as inheritance law is outdated and does not reflect present-day family set-ups.

If you inherit money or property from an unmarried partner, you are not exempt from paying IHT, as married couples are. You are liable for any debts in your own name, but not for any debts that are just in your partner's name. You may be responsible for debts in joint names and for others for which you have 'joint and several' legal responsibility.

Even if you have successfully navigated the intricacies of being financially even-handed during life, you could inadvertently leave your loved ones with difficulties after death. The most nuclear of families can implode following the death of a parent if the will does not contain what all the offspring were expecting. And when there are children from different relationships, and stepchildren too, there are many more opportunities for stress. This can cause challenges to wills.

MARLENE AND RICHARD

I remember when my husband and I made our wills; we had both been married before with children from those marriages, though we had no children together. Richard had two daughters and I one. Now those daughters have six grandchildren between them. We had our own assets and joint ones, and I own a business of which my daughter is a director and sits on the board. Our starting point was that we wanted to be fair. Over the years we have been generous with all our children, funding them through university, helping them to buy and improve homes and setting up education trusts for their children.

At all times, we have maintained the gifts as equally as possible.

Who should benefit from my business was a tricky part of the discussion. My stepdaughters have no interest in the business, nor would they want any, and they live too far away to play an active part in it, whereas my daughter is fully cognizant of the business operation and would know how to keep running it. The value is a large part of my estate – how could I be fair if I were leaving it solely to my daughter? Of course, having a conversation with all three children might prompt a solution. The two stepdaughters might say it was quite fair to leave them no share in my business. They might not expect to receive a share of it. However, if I sell the business or take it public before I die, do I share some of my money with them then?

Be in no doubt that the area of inheritance and wills is emotional and therefore difficult. Some things intricately bind money and support with affection and value – even when that is not the case and not what you intended. Ensure you have made good provision for yourself and your partner before deciding who should inherit what. To put safeguards in place may mean changing or sharing ownership of some assets. Until you have clarified what it is you and your partner want and need, the mechanisms by which you ensure who gets what share of your estate after you die (trusts and other approaches I will discuss in Chapter Four) are not a prime consideration.

The basic principle in England and Wales is that you are free to make a will that leaves your assets to whoever you choose. Flexibility in your affairs will make that easier. Although that may resolve some of these difficulties, making the choices is that much harder.

Civil partnerships and unmarried couples

Your relationship with your partner is key to sorting out your succession planning and you need to be clear about your position before taking any action.

In the section about blended families I mentioned in passing unmarried couples and civil partnerships. I have brought them together in this section because, while the legal rights of civil partners and married couples are largely the same, there are some important differences; and there are some significant differences between the rights of unmarried couples and of those that have tied the knot.

Originally the law established civil partnerships for same-sex partners but they are now open to partners of different sex. Civil partnerships and marriage offer couples the same rights over property and pensions, and the tax allowances available to couples in a civil partnership are the same as those for married couples. The key variances between the two types of union come down to the formalities that need to be carried out when they begin or when they end.

To enter a marriage, a marriage certificate needs to be issued and this can now contain the names of both parents of each partner (previously only their fathers were named), after legal changes to the process came into force. The same is true for a civil partnership. The change is part of a new digital system to modernise, simplify and speed up the process for registering marriages and partnerships, helping to tackle a backlog. It formalised a civil partnership through the signing of a document called the schedule of civil partnership. This is different to marriage, which is validated by each person saying a set of prescribed words: making 'vows'. Civil partnerships have no religious grounding; they are entirely secular. Marriages can be celebrated in a religious ceremony (although some religions do not recognise same-sex marriages) but are now established in the secular realm (by a register office issuing a marriage certificate).

If you are in a civil partnership, you cannot legally say that you are 'married'. Same-sex couples can become civil partners, and can now convert a civil partnership into a marriage in England or Wales.[22] Once you have registered a civil partnership, it ends if one of you dies, or you apply to court to bring the partnership to a legal end, and you cannot do this until the partnership has lasted for at least one year. However, the grounds ending a partnership are like those for divorce.

As civil partners, you may choose to draw up an agreement, known as a pre-registration agreement, before you register your partnership. This can set out your rights and obligations towards each other and what should happen if your relationship breaks down. It can include arrangements for children and your personal possessions, for example the family home and any pensions. It is not legally binding but could influence the courts if your partnership breaks down and they get involved. One of the biggest incentives for couples to enter a civil partnership is to secure inheritance rights. Cohabiting and unmarried couples have serious disadvantages under the present inheritance rules; here is why.

Under current law, if you and your partner live together without marrying you cannot automatically inherit each other's assets. This means that, on death, the surviving partner receives nothing under the intestacy rules, where there is no will. In contrast, if you are married or have a civil partner you may receive their assets under the intestacy rules when they die. Therefore, it is crucial to write a will, to be more certain that your partner will inherit your estate.

When one cohabiting partner dies without leaving a will, the surviving partner may claim from their estate through the Inheritance (Provision for Family and Dependants) Act 1975.[23] Surviving unmarried partners can apply through the Act for provision from their deceased partner's estate. They may make a claim under the Act if:

- Their partner died intestate (without a will).

- Their partner left a will but did not adequately provide for the surviving partner within it.

If you are neither married nor in a civil partnership, but cohabiting with your partner, no matter for how long, there is no other law to protect you on death, except a will. Like civil partners, you can make an official agreement if you want to set down your legal rights in certain areas of your relationship with your partner that the courts will recognise (these are known as living together agreements or cohabitation contracts). Such an agreement could cover, for example, shared responsibility for your children, ownership of property which you live in and joint ownership of possessions. Although the courts recognise these, it may be difficult to force your partner to keep to the terms of them.

If a married couple or in a civil partnership you can inherit your partner's ISA investments and benefit from death benefits from a Defined Benefit Pension Scheme. The law does not extend these rights to unmarried couples who live together, which seems mightily unfair in today's day and age (some pension schemes' rules do recognise unmarried couples). In addition, you cannot claim a state retirement pension based on your partner's National Insurance contributions.

The biggest problem for unmarried couples is that, when one of you dies, there could be an IHT bill. On death your IHT is not charged on assets passing to a surviving spouse or civil partner, and it is also possible to transfer any unused IHT allowances from your deceased spouse or civil partner. Neither of these IHT benefits are available to unmarried couples. If your partner's will leaves their estate to you but it is worth more than £325,000 (the NRB – see Chapter Two), you will pay tax on the excess. So, for instance, if your partner leaves an estate worth £500,000, then £325,000 you pay no tax on, leaving £175,000, which is taxed at 40%, giving you a tax bill of £70,000.

If you have children, whatever your status, provided you have left your principal residence to your children in your will there is the RNRB (£175,000 at date of writing)[24] which you can offset against the value of the property only. However, complications arise for unmarried couples where your cohabitee owns the home jointly with you: on your death it does not pass to your children, so they lose this allowance.

It is not unusual for couples to agree on everything. Many people readily write mutual wills, in which they leave all they own first to one another and on the second death, split it equally between the children. But one person may want to give to their children while still living and the other may want to wait until death. If those wills do not really allow for that, a fresh approach will be necessary.

If your cohabitee leaves their share of the family home to their own children, their estate will benefit from the RNRB – but it will rarely be desirable that the children become co-owners with the survivor (even if the survivor is also a parent). A child could run into financial difficulties or go through a divorce – and their ownership of the inherited share could put the survivor at risk of losing their home.

The probable answer is to get married, but there may be all kinds of reasons this does not happen.

To cascade your wealth and pass it to your chosen beneficiaries, you can see that there is more to do than just write a will. Although that is necessary, there are several issues to contemplate. As you will read in the next section, discussion and conversations with family members can do much to resolve some of these issues.

The older generation

While it is automatic to think about the next generation when considering how to pass on your wealth, it can sometimes be easy to forget the impact of the older generation, even if they are physically fit and well.

Factoring in the influence that your parents or other older relatives may have on your plans is of paramount importance. Lifestyle changes and medical breakthroughs have been on the increase over the years. This may mean that your family, parents, uncles, aunts are living longer, leading more active lives than generations before theirs. This, in turn, may mean that they have funds to pass on. However, like you, they must do a certain amount of planning to ensure they have enough money for their own needs first. While your family may be elderly, maybe they are still living independently and in relatively good health.

All that can change, in an instance. We have only to look at the effects of the COVID-19 pandemic to see this. Apart from that, there is no getting away from the fact that as we age, we become less mobile, less able and far slower. If poor physical health does not affect ageing parents, then dementia could. As a result, one of or both your parents could end up paying an enormous amount for care. While an inheritance for you might appear likely, costs of care can eat into this rapidly.

CASE STUDY: DOES THE HOME PAY FOR CARE COSTS?

Thomas spent most of his working life paying the mortgage on the home he and his wife, Maisie, bought from a private landlord. Thomas wanted to ensure that on his death he would have paid it off. It was likely he would die before Maisie, having been a Japanese prisoner of war and with some serious medical ailments as a result, and sadly he did. Maisie eventually ended up in a care home because of dementia, and much of the equity in the family home was used to pay for care costs. I doubt Thomas had ever considered that this was where his hard-earned money would eventually end up. It limited their children's inheritance, but it provided for good care.

If relatives do not qualify for local authority financial support, you would want them to have the best of care and help find the means to finance it, such as selling or renting their home. But this may be a tough conversation to have with your parents, especially if they cannot see the problems themselves. Their needs might demand more practical physical care and support if they remain in their home. This gives little time for you to focus on your own needs, and those of the next generation. Recognising the needs of an older generation should urge you to make good preparation for your own old age, particularly through retaining access to wealth. As we live longer, it is quite typical for several generations in a family to be alive and well:

- In the next twenty years, the number of older people in England is projected to rise:

  - For those aged 65 years and older – by nearly 50%

  - For those aged 85 years and older – by 114%.

- Nearly one in five people currently in the UK will live to see their 100th birthday.[25]

So, it is the overall intergenerational outlook that you should focus on; each generation is distinct and has differing requirements, outlooks, attitudes, values and approach to money. You need also to take a view on how the total wealth of a family can work for everyone while making sure they are fulfilling and satisfying their own needs.

I am sure you find the anticipation of arranging for care or for your death uncomfortable topics. Many of us try not to think about these thorny and sensitive subjects unless forced to. It is often worth broaching the subject and dealing with any initial discomfort to get the potential rewards of effective wealth transfer planning. By looking both forwards and backwards, you view your family in its entirety. Rather than focusing just on your own wealth in isolation, you can now involve all members of the family, who will experience different financial challenges simultaneously.

How to get people talking and in discussion will probably be one of your biggest challenges. If you have been a family that does not talk about money openly, it is going to be a difficult and uphill climb. For some, money is harder to talk about than death. There are going to be some awkward moments. Your parents might suspect you of ulterior motives, so it is better to introduce the subject gently. You do not have to put all your assets or burdens on the table or ask outright what your parents' intentions are for their old age and their demise. A neutral location is best, such as a restaurant or hotel, but somewhere you can have confidential discussions between as many family members as possible.

It helps if you have a rational idea of your agenda, remain calm and carry on and listen to everyone's views. Be open. It is not a family summit and you do not have to make far-reaching decisions at this stage. It will be helpful enough to have opened the subject, get a feel for how people are with it and what their views are. Most importantly, do not be judgemental or this could lead to arguments and possibly close the topic altogether. Remember, older people may see money and giving it as a sign of affection, but younger ones may see this as exerting control or influence.

Understanding and respecting everyone's views will be critical, so open-ended questions and talking tentatively will help the conversation and hopefully bring the desired result. Providing everyone with space to air how they feel and what they want, from youngest to oldest, helps empower them and may give them the feeling that they are playing an important part.

Rather than focusing on the wealthiest generation individually, there will be opportunities to help all members of the family, who will experience different financial challenges simultaneously. Later you can see what roles everyone can play and assist with any issues that may arise. Young people are often happy and willing to help their grandparents, run errands, read stories, go for walks, get involved in many activities. It does not all have to fall on your shoulders and the older people in your life will more than welcome the chance to see more of their family, I am sure.

You want this to be just the start of many discussions, in which ultimately each generation can appreciate and understand the wealth or care plans of the others and how they should deal with them.

Being able to carry out their wishes on your parents' death is probably the greatest service you can perform for them. Doesn't that make you think you can continue with the same momentum and adopt a similar approach with your other loved ones in cascading your wealth?

Religion and culture

You may need some sensitivity towards these issues if they matter to you or other family members and friends.

If you wish to imbue estate-planning documents with religious values or to transmit a particular religious heritage to heirs, one of the most important decisions is the selection of executors and/or trustees, and this should have some of the following characteristics:

• They must know the faith.

- They will probably be affiliated to or observe the faith themselves.

- They must show sensitivity to the specific needs of the heirs, considering your religious goals and objectives.

Perhaps the person who best fits these criteria will not be best suited to handle investment and other financial responsibilities, so this combination might need to be sought from more than one individual. It might be possible to name one person to be a trust protector who can oversee certain, say religious, issues and another to fulfil general duties as executor or trustee. If this is an area of concern or importance, then you should seek guidance or discussion over how to grant legal authority, for example to disburse funds for religious education (perhaps supplemental religious education or private schooling), religious travel (pilgrimages to holy sites), charitable giving (to instruct heirs in core religious values) and other purposes associated with your religious or cultural goals.

According to Martin M Shenkman, many religions encourage charitable giving to reflect the distinct requirements of a particular faith. Although many religions suggest covenanting a percentage of your income or assets to charity, some lay out more specific criteria while others, such as the Mormon faith, provide guidance but leave much to personal choice. Shenkman explains that charitable giving is an essential part of the Bahá'í faith, as this shows devotion to

Bohol and represents the ideal of charity. Bahá'ís are expected to give a certain percentage of their incomes and assets to Bahá'í charitable organisations through a mandatory donation referred to as Ḥuqúqu'lláh ('the right of God'). Shenkman notes that it is common for members of this and other faiths to make bequests in their wills to charity, give agents financial Powers of Attorney to make charitable gifts on their behalf and, perhaps, include charitable beneficiaries in trusts:

> A secular will may have to be changed to reflect the Bahá'í, Jewish, Islamic, or other religious laws of inheritance. Both the Koran and Old Testament include detailed provisions on how you should handle inheritance. Although similar, they typically apply quite different manners in will drafting. These provisions need to be coordinated with tax, estate, financial and succession planning, as well as ethical issues. For the Orthodox Christian, if the believer does not provide for their family and relatives, it is as if you have disowned the faith and are worse than a nonbeliever. If you are a Catholic, you know that there are general guidelines of charity and justice to be respected.[26]

Buddhism advocates that believers act out of compassion and not anger and that any form of estate planning be about more than just the transmission of wealth: for many, it should encompass the transmission of beliefs and values. You can achieve this by integrating religious considerations into the estate-planning process.

One example of this is where you have minor children. You may wish to ensure that funds are available for religious schooling. Some religions have specific instructions about how property should be divided between heirs and others have prohibitions on charging interest that might apply to transactions the estate is allowed to make. As there are many religions and different levels of belief, it is impossible to list every example.

What does all this mean to you? If you want to make sure you reflect your religious beliefs in your estate plan, then you should factor this into your planning and ensure that the professionals who act for you, such as a solicitor drafting your will, are aware of your requirements.

Likewise, a family's behaviour or culture can affect how you design your Family Wealth Plan. Different family cultures require different estate-planning structures. Creating estate-planning structures that match your family culture is critical. Identifying misalignment between culture and structure can help families – in collaboration with the professional team – understand the importance of preparation for the plans that you create. Doing this can help avoid or mitigate a range of potential problems, from family legal battles to untoward effects of too much wealth, by promoting positive family interactions and outcomes.

For example, a principle of Chinese inheritance law is that a first level of successor(s) shall inherit to the exclusion of any successor(s) second in order. Only when there is no successor at the first level does the right of inheritance pass to the successor(s) of the second level. Moreover, successors at the same level must inherit in equal shares. So, if a foreigner living in China passes away, then under Chinese law they must share property between this person's surviving spouse, children and parents.[27]

While in principle spouse, children and parents share equally, Chinese law also establishes another principle, that assets are jointly owned by the husband and wife. So, if one passes, how should they divide assets among the spouse, children and parents?

If there is any misalignment, then you can work to correct it. The easiest way is to simplify the planning to match the capabilities and competences of family members. Accordingly, is it important *in your family* to preserve wealth, to grow it, to divide it up equally, to give some to charity or to use it to develop others; even use a combination of these? Chances are you may not know or even be concerned about this, but at least it warrants some consideration.

In a survey carried out by Merrill,[28] more than a quarter of participants noted that taking care of and handling money wisely were top concerns. As you consider your own estate plan and weigh the importance of communicating about stewardship, what pathway resonates most with you?

- 45% **Preservation** – assets passing to the beneficiaries using professional management designed to minimise estate taxation and provide a flow of assets.

- 22% **Division** – beneficiaries receiving a fixed amount, with any outstanding balance being passed to a charitable institution.

- 17% **Growth** – beneficiaries directly managing wealth.

- 16% **Undecided** – still waiting to decide on future steps.

Family traditions can be as important as any legal documents when distributing your wealth. Relationships and backgrounds can be preserved and protected in any estate planning. Who inherits and manages, how and when you make transfers, and what restrictions you place on each aspect, essentially preserves and protects the intangible aspects most important to you – your legacy, your traditions and your values. Trusts and wills, etc are merely devices that let these stories endure.

Summary

Facing the various challenges and obstacles leaves you free to open your mind to other ideas. Holding discussions with the people you intend to inherit your wealth provides clarity and greater certainty for all. This paves the way for a better understanding of your family's needs and frees you to examine the possibility of other openings.

Do not see these discussions as obstacles, but as opportunities to achieve your goals and objectives, while satisfying others' needs and demands.

FOUR

L Is About Laying
The Foundations

You should now be able to make the most of the options that may be available to you. Again, the focus is on family members and the part they can play in cementing your Family Wealth Plan. Now you can grasp every opportunity to help the next generation, whether family or friends, to benefit from your knowledge and experience. You are the person who can help them understand the part they play in your Family Wealth Plan. How they deal with matters on your death, what they can expect and the roles and responsibilities they may have to employ can benefit from your guidance.

Intergenerational wealth

There is a Chinese belief that wealth only lasts for three generations, if you are lucky, and that most times only for two. In the USA, only 12% of family businesses continue into the third generation.[29] This can be put down to lack of careful planning and not considering what we have discussed thus far. Often, though, it can be just lack of understanding on both sides: what the next generation want, what their values, missions, attitudes and agenda are as opposed to yours. Have you ever stopped to think how significantly different these may be from your own, even if on the surface you seem to share the same family culture?

Death and distribution of assets are not topics that you can raise easily at dinner, or when your children drop in with the grandchildren, who will demand time and attention. Their own family problems may be preoccupation enough, without wanting to think about yours.

Clients often tell me that when they mention dividing up the estate, their children dismiss the idea quickly, saying they should just spend their money on them-selves. That is fine and good to hear, but it does not solve any problems. If you find it hard enough to face up to your own mortality, then you will also have trouble opening a conversation about passing on your wealth after your death. As I have acknowl-edged, it is not the easiest of subjects to broach. When you do, there can be so many issues to consider, so many options, that it is easy to put the subject off to the future.

Hopefully, as you work your way through this book, you will have come to the stage where you have taken stock, worked out what you own and what you need for the rest of your lifetime; you have hopefully given thought to how any legacies you leave will affect your beneficiaries, individually and together. You should now think seriously about the actions you will take during the next few years and what you will write in your will, so that they can carry out your wishes.

You may already help your children but feel you could do more. While your children may be grateful for the financial support, there are those who will be defiantly independent and want to achieve their objectives on their own. Understanding the different generations is a good point from which to start to pass on intergenerational wealth. Your own family may not be stereotypical, but there will be aspects of it that will shed light on how best to pass on some of your wealth.

There is a good section on this in my book *Boomers: Redefining Retirement*,[30] so I will only summarise the main considerations here.

Those born after the baby boom, between the mid-1960s and late 1980s, make up the generation now known as Generation X. As adolescents and young adults they were often called the 'MTV Generation' and characterised as slackers and as cynical and disaffected. In mid-life, research describes Generation X adults as active, happy and achieving a work–life balance. Many have entrepreneurial tendencies. They have, however, learned to embrace and be more open to diversity. With that said, a 'what's in it for me' attitude has prevailed. They are certainly better educated and more decisive than their parents.

Generation Y or the Millennials were born between the 1980s and the year 2000. I would include my children in this group; they have grown up with technology, accustomed to gadgets and social media. They feel less fortunate than you, although some, possibly with your help, have bought their own homes. But they have not had access to the guaranteed pensions and the continuity of employment that can contribute to the accumulation of capital.

Certainly, we helped fund our children through university, bought their first car, helped them with deposits for a house and, over the years, with other financial support. None of it they have asked for, mind you, but all was thankfully received.

Generation Z was born in the 1990s to early in the present century. While they are living in an age of high-tech communication, technology-driven lifestyles and prolific use of social media, like their parents they tend to be more enterprising, to plan more and to have a greater global outlook.

Sometimes, the next generation rarely understand the blood, sweat and tears that created wealth, or even do not understand the value of money. It does not motivate some heirs to develop a bias towards diligence, thrift or delayed gratification or build the relationships with others who contribute to wealth accumulation. Do you recognise any of your children here, or even your grandchildren? How do you think they will appreciate and use the money that you give to them? Maybe you are fearful that they will blow your hard-earned money on fast cars and easy living. Alternatively, they could be prudent and invest some of it, pass some on to their own family, use it to start a business or just get rid of debts. Unless you know them well or have the discussions, you will be none the wiser and led by your own preconceptions or assumptions.

Start a serious conversation with the younger ones about their hopes and dreams. Getting to know your family well and understanding what they want from life can assist you with your own planning. Are there likely to be more grandchildren or great-grandchildren to consider in the future? If there is a family business, do not assume your children will want to be part of it and take it over after you.

How well do you and your family members get on and communicate? Remember, while you may pass on wisdom and riches to the next generation, they can teach you too and surprise you with their expertise, abilities and wisdom. There is nothing better than sharing ideals and knowledge.

Inheritance now or later?

The most obvious action to take for your children, especially younger ones who might not have the maturity to deal with large amounts of money, is to make investments on their behalf. You may have already set up a few, such as child trust funds (when they were about), Junior ISAs maybe and you may even have gone so far as setting up a trust.

There are many benefits of gifting your inheritance to your adult children during your life rather than waiting for it to be passed on in your will, which can be a rather more solemn matter. You will be around to see the enormous difference your gift is going to make to the lives of your loved ones. This will mean that you can enjoy it with them, and this can be a happy affair, adventure or experience, depending on the gift (it does not have to be pounds and pence). Young adults in their early 20s and 30s may feel the benefit most, because this can be when they have just started up the ladder of their career, just got married or moved in with a partner. In any of these circumstances, they might have recently bought or be thinking of buying a home. There could even be children around or on the horizon. Some may be in business or just starting up, and financial help at the beginning could make a significant difference; so a gift at this stage of their life could be huge for them.

If you leave it in your will, then no doubt they will be older, may already have paid off their mortgage but not be in any actual need of the money. It could then end up being passed to their children or beneficiaries, but more crucially adding to their IHT bill. Since people are living longer, there are many octogenarians and nonagenarians, which could mean that the children we are discussing might even be in their 60s and 70s and thinking about their own wealth planning.

Gifting now could mean saving your family IHT, especially if you use exemptions and survive the gift by seven years. I will go into these in more detail in Chapter Five.

As I mentioned earlier, you may be concerned that someone will not spend wisely but use the money too quickly or squander it. This makes planning and preparation, and communicating with your family, of paramount importance. Gifting before a person is ready to deal with the gift could do more harm than good. Setting up a trust is one way to protect wealth through the generations. A trust can be as specific or descriptive as you wish, and you can appoint people, members of your family perhaps, whom you can trust to carry out your wishes. While gifting into trust can eventually save tax, its real value is in the protection it offers to future generations from financial repercussions of death, disability or divorce. Using a trust will help you make individualised plans if necessary – to arrange for a child with health problems or to provide for one who might be better off not inheriting a lump sum. It can also help you give more to the child who did most of the work of caring for you in your later years or less to the one whose extensive education you funded while paying far less towards their siblings' education.

However, I would like to share some insights into what your inheritors may feel or how they might behave when they receive your generous gift. First, they probably are expecting something more or less than what they receive. They probably do not know how wealthy you are, beyond the value of your home, especially if you do not have a lavish lifestyle. Younger people rarely realise that relatives living frugally and spending wisely may have accumulated wealth. Conversely, extravagance and rich living can make you wealthy during your lifetime, but leave little when you die.

Repeatedly, clients have requested advice for elderly family members who have amassed considerable wealth and are unsure how to deal with it. They are usually acting under Powers of Attorney for relatives who have gone into care and can no longer take responsibility for the money. The reality of this, the technicalities and tax implications that go along with it, can overwhelm them, especially if there is a broad range of assets – cash, property, investments, land, other valuables such as antiques, art collections and jewellery, to name but a few.

The boomer generation has a lot of wealth to hand down now and in coming years, which suggests that the next cohorts might see a boost to their standards of living. There are several positive aspects to inter-generational wealth transfers:

- The amounts of wealth involved

- The owners may use little of it during their lifetime

- It will include one or more homes, even property portfolios

- Inheritance is a growing cycle

However, without a Family Wealth Plan, you might transfer wealth too late to help the next branch of the family or even the one after that. Many Millennials cannot afford to own their own property, and when they inherit from you it may come too late to help them support their living standards during what can be an expensive family stage.

Education

It is not just assets that you can share with your inheritors; here is a great opportunity to educate them, whatever their age. If they are not financially savvy and they are going to receive sizeable sums of money, you need to ensure that they will be able to manage it. You can help them understand where they stand tax-wise and what might be the best way to handle their new wealth.

If finance has not been a subject on the school curriculum (and with some schools, it may not have been), then it is never too soon to start. Older children may have already picked up some understanding from parents or peers, some will be naturally interested and maybe pursuing careers in finance. It does not follow that they have a real grasp on making money work for them to achieve their goals and objectives.

In much the same way as I have been advocating that you develop your Family Wealth Plan to deal with the handing over of your estate, I hope you can recommend to your children to get on a sound financial footing and look forwards. This will teach them budgeting, while familiarising them with the value of what they buy.

For a few years, my company took part in 'My Money Week', an event that took us into junior schools to provide some financial education. It was great fun, if not especially demanding, to help young people gain the skills, knowledge and confidence in money matters to thrive in society. 'My Money Week' is a brilliant scheme as it ensures learners grow to understand their attitude to risk and realise their own behaviour and emotions when making financial decisions through real-life scenarios.

Will your younger generation recognise the impact of debt, liabilities and credit scoring, and how these can affect their future? We are a more cashless society. I recall worrying that, when my daughter was a child, she would think that money came out of holes in the wall. I was much happier when I could give her an allowance each month, laying down what I expected her to buy and seeing how long her funds would last. Even giving a child a piggy bank, in which they can see the money piling up, is a simple but great incentive.

Equipping children and young adults with the skills and knowledge they need to make well-informed financial decisions and to engage with the financial services sector can only add to their confidence as they make their way through life.

One of the biggest ways children learn is by observing. Chances are, you go to work to provide for your family. Your child can see that a relationship exists between work and money. Have a conversation with a child about work and how your earnings influence your purchases, where you live and how you get to work. Having conversations about your work, how you started and progressed, and what a difference it made to your lifestyle is a great lesson. Another great way to teach your children about money is by including them when paying bills or discussing large purchases. Family financial meetings can be a way of teaching them about the financial choices you make, and why you decide a certain way. Depending on their age, try to put it in terms they understand. The key idea is to teach them the importance of budgets and making choices with money.

Children learn about money by doing. By having them actively take part in a trip to the supermarket and sharing the experience with them, getting them to choose goods by price, for example, they can see how budgeting relates to shopping. Getting them to open a savings account online provides an opportunity to teach them about saving money. The Go Henry card is a great way for children to accept gifts from the family, and seeing the money accumulate online can make them less eager to spend it. My grandson's money goal, when he got a card, was to save £100 within a year. He was banking on some generous relatives; but instead of buying lots of plastic toys, which often children discard within hours, you can give some money to the plastic card which they can then spend on the next family shopping trip or excursion. If an older child dog-sits, or babysits, you can use these occasions to teach about earning, spending, saving and donating.

Children can learn about money by reading with you. There are children's books which teach all about earning, spending, saving, borrowing and donating. These books provide an easy and spontaneous opportunity for questions and answers. Children also learn about money by playing, particularly if you join in with them. Board games with play money such as Monopoly can be influential teachers. Online games provide a fun way to teach about money and start smart money conversations.

Once in their teens, children should be able to handle themselves and better understand the difference between needs and wants. They may have access to more money, but probably they also want more. It is now that they need to learn how to prioritise, but learning can be a demanding process. They may be more aware of the need to save, especially if you are giving them pocket money or they are earning a little themselves. The experiences they had and habits they picked up early in life can dominate their attitude to money. How parents, family, teachers and friends have influenced them will contribute to these. The conversations about money will be the most helpful and teach them greater responsibility.

Students can quickly learn about debt and paying their way through university. However, if they are supported and somewhat cushioned by the bank of mum and dad (and a student loan, which they do not have to repay until they earn a reasonable wage), this can leave them a little naïve. So the communication about money should not stop as children grow into adulthood. It is surprising how the money word is taboo in many families, even between partners. The psychological impact of this in their own relationships may continue. Money is an emotive word and has different connotations for us all, so start with this closing message. What does it mean to you?

Roles and responsibilities

During your lifetime, some actions I am advocating will have involved you in appointing executors of your will, giving Powers of Attorney to act on your behalf and appointing trustees to administer any trusts. You may have asked your family and friends to perform these roles. They might have willingly obliged, perhaps without really understanding the demands and effort required of them.

Some of you may appoint professionals, such as solicitors, and this can be helpful as you instruct the practice, not the individual and you know well who signs the documents. Having the legal profession involved has its pluses and minuses. On one hand, they might be familiar with the legalities and able to deal with any issue such as a will being contested; ad hoc payments from your accounts or trusts, which may be necessary; or, if things go amiss, with the Court of Protection. However, you need to be sure they will still be around in many years' time, so the larger the practice, the better. It can take a long time to deal with paperwork and courts. You have the reassurance that they have some information about you and your ultimate wishes after your death, so should ensure that they duly carry them out.

In your personal papers or will, you might recommend a firm of lawyers for your family to deal with, that they can consider when the time comes. If a member wants, say, to relinquish the role as an executor, they can hand it over to the lawyers.

The other problem you may have in choosing a solicitor is that they may not be expert estate practitioners. You need an experienced specialist who can deal with matters with compassion and understanding. So, make sure you choose a lawyer or a firm with the right expertise at outset. There are other excellent alternatives to solicitors, such as estate administrators.

You might end up handing various roles and responsibilities to people who not only are not professionals but are complete novices in this area of work. They may find it difficult to understand the jargon, the intricacies and the bureaucracy they will have to deal with. Learning and navigating this takes time and much patience. The roles need not be difficult, but it would pay you to pass on some information and steps they can follow which will leave no ambiguities. It will be hard enough for them to deal with your death, so a little forethought will go a long way and I am sure be appreciated by those to whom you give these tasks.

I will start first with the people you select to give Powers of Attorney. (For this purpose, they are called 'attorneys' though you may not have appointed lawyers to do this.) I will not go into the details of the documents here, other than to say that there are two types, enduring and lasting. You might have one, both or neither, and I would advise you to attend to that immediately. For a friend or family member to be your attorney is an important duty and not to be carried out lightly. For one thing, they must be able to communicate easily and promptly. So, having two people who hardly know each other and live at opposite ends of the country might not work well. They will need to know your wishes, so do not wait until you lose capacity to show them the contents of the power, which they may have signed without full cognizance of what they will be undertaking. Make sure you give them information (easily available from the internet) about the general responsibilities and what can be expected of them.

A power ends when you do; you may still have all your faculties, but have decided to hand responsibility to your attorneys. They are then accountable for your financial matters, or your health and welfare, and these can seem heavy responsibilities. This can lead to worrying times, so being crystal-clear at the outset about what you want is the order of the day.

Then there are the executors who will carry out the instructions in your will. They can be the same people as your attorneys; or a professional you appoint; or a board of a professional, an attorney and one or more relatives. You may appoint from one to four executors. It would pay to have at least two in case something happens to one of them after you sign the will. Having too many could lead to delays, especially if they do not live near one another. If one of them cannot be contacted, there must be proof that someone tried to contact them, or it will be impossible to appoint a replacement.

If you are married or living with someone, you will often appoint your partner an executor, but you can appoint anyone over the age of 18 years. Executors must be people you can trust. They will have the job of gathering all the information about the assets you own, so make it easy for them. Having a Family Wealth Plan means that all the information is readily accessible and easy to understand. Theirs is the job of identifying and contacting professional bodies, assessing your assets' value and obtaining market valuations for any land or property. If you have assets abroad, then they will have to deal with those too, and probably a lawyer in that country. Hopefully, you will have made a will in that country, too, as part of your Family Wealth Plan.

Let your executors have a copy of your will, even talk them through it. They need to know that they may have to pay any taxes, settle any debts and distribute the estate to the beneficiaries (even have to track beneficiaries down). It will be important for them to keep records in case of any disputes or disagreements. If your chosen executor(s) feels it might all be too much or you cannot appoint anyone suitable, then you can ask a solicitor or accountant instead. The fees they charge may save your family anxious time and effort, or even save money elsewhere.

You can find details of the duties of executors online.[31]

Finally, if you set up trusts to look after any part of your estate you need to appoint trustees. Again, trustees can also be your attorney(s) or executor(s), but they have specific duties laid down in the trusts you set up. Their job is to look after the assets of the trust and pay out income or capital to the beneficiaries named in the trust. I discuss this in more detail in Chapter Five.

People to whom you delegate authority may be close to you, so may not be in the right state of mind to deal with the demands that are put on them when you die. They will have their own grief to deal with. It would be easy for them to make mistakes or fail to follow the rules properly, no matter how well meaning. You can help them by making the right decisions now, not only in your appointments but in making sure they have the necessary information to act on your behalf.

Summary

Laying the foundations involves more than just passing on your wealth. It is about the exchange of knowledge and sharing of information. If your family lives far and wide, there is now the technology to link up with them to have the desired conversations, even to record them. Sharing information and documents is relatively easy but, whatever else you do, send copies by post to the people you appoint to carry out your wishes. There can be no excuse for not communicating some of the ideas we have discussed, learning from other potential beneficiaries and explaining the different roles and responsibilities.

FIVE

Other Options

It may not be possible to carry out every single action I recommend or follow my advice, for various reasons. The Family Wealth Plan needs to be tailored to you, your circumstances and those of your family. By this stage you should have implemented some of your plan. However, there are still some options for cascading your wealth to consider:

- IHT exemptions

- Charitable donations

- Allowances and reliefs

- Trusts

If you have decided that you want to mitigate as much inheritance tax as possible while you still have time, then this chapter should help you.

Making use of IHT exemptions

Armed with knowledge about how to avoid IHT legitimately, you can decide which approaches would be the best for you and your inheritors.

So, starting small, you can assess which exemptions that you and any partner could use each year that would probably not tax you too much (excuse the pun). Exemptions are the small gifts you can make which will be free of the tax immediately. You do not have to survive the gifts by seven years, as with larger gifts, but you must not benefit from them either. Every individual has an exemption of £3,000 a year. If you did not use this in the previous tax year, you can carry it forward one year (but only once). By now your Family Wealth Plan will show you whether you have sufficient uncommitted income or capital to use this exemption.

You can also make exempt gifts 'in contemplation of' marriage or civil partnership:

- Up to £5,000 can be given by each parent.
- Up to £2,500 can be given by each grandparent or remoter ancestor.

- Up to £1,000 can be given by any person.

- Up to £2,500 can be given by one partner to the other.

In addition, you can give £250 to many people, or you can make regular gifts from income, but to claim this allowance, you need to meet three conditions:

- Each gift must form part of your normal expenditure.

- It must come from your income and not capital.

- It must not leave you without sufficient income to maintain your normal standard of living.

It is best to keep a record of these payments, in case HMRC requires your executors to show that you met the conditions. Again, your Family Wealth Plan will show you whether you can support this. All the gifts can be to the same person, but if you have already given them £3,000 you are not allowed to use this exemption to give that person additional amounts.

One useful way of using this exemption is to set up a life policy. Most people use a 'whole of life' plan to cover the potential IHT on their estate. If a married couple or in a registered civil partnership, it pays out the sum assured on the second death, ie when the executor must calculate any tax liability. Putting the plan in trust places the policy outside your estate immediately and this means the money can be paid to your beneficiaries without waiting for probate, enabling them to pay the tax straight away. The payment is tax free.

You may dislike life assurance. Maybe you think the premiums too high: they will depend on your age and state of health. However, I believe this to be an optimal approach for many people. It means they no longer need worry about their dependants having to pay IHT, so can use their assets or give them freely without worry. If tax rates fall and the policy pays out more than needed, all you are doing is giving your family more money, tax free; if they rise, you can increase the cover; even if you did not manage to do this, at worst your family would only have to find the difference, not the whole tax bill.

Putting life policies into trust is a relatively inexpensive way of avoiding IHT, provided you take advice. You will need people to act as your trustees. They will have to sign any documentation, along with yourself.

Although maintenance for family members is not strictly exempted, gifts made to do this, ie to a spouse/civil partner, minor children, children in full-time education and/or relatives financially dependent on you do not attract IHT, so no liability will arise.

What makes up a gift? It can be anything that has a value (such as money, property, possessions) or represents a loss in the value of your estate when it is transferred (for example, if you sell your house to your child for less than it is worth, the difference in value counts as a gift).

Be aware, though, that the exemptions apply to gifts in date order, so gifts made earlier in the tax year will benefit from an exemption before later ones. If you make donations on the same day, you will need to share the exemptions among them.

To sum up, using income or capital superfluous to your needs reduces your estate and thus the tax bill for your beneficiaries; not spending superfluous money means you are adding to them.

Here are some ideas to consider if you wish to use the exemptions:

- Give directly to an individual or several people you know and let them decide how to use the gift.

- Purchase an item then give it.

- Put money into trust, again as a one-off, or every month or year.

- Start paying university or education fees.

- Pay off debts, for example on credit cards.

- Invest money on your inheritors' behalf in savings, investments, pensions as a single payment or regularly.

While a Junior Individual Savings Account (JISA) needs to be set up by the child's parent or legal guardian, anyone can pay into the account later. The child has full access to the money at age 18, so it may not be appropriate in every case, but all income and gains on the underlying investments are tax free. Grandparents might want to pay some money into their grandchildren's JISAs, but these payments are 'potentially exempt transfers' (PETs), unless made under the annual exemption of £3,000, which can be contributed without the seven-year time limit that applies to PETs.

Likewise, pensions attract tax-free growth, and you can contribute on behalf of a child (or adult who has no earnings), a maximum of £3,600 each year (compared to the exempt gifts of £3,000 gross or gifts out of normal income). With tax relief at 20%, the net cost to you is £2,880. If the adult member is a higher-rate taxpayer, they will be able to reclaim additional relief through their tax return.

Do take care that, if anyone you donate to is claiming state benefits or grants, your regular gifts (or, indeed, a lump sum) do not take them over an income or capital threshold and so would have to be declared. For example, currently a person may not claim income support if they have more than £16,000 in capital.

There is no income tax for your family to pay on any gifts you make, though there might be tax implications for interest or dividends received on any savings or investments that are not tax free (unlike (J)ISAs or pensions).

Political donations can be exempt under certain conditions.

In purely monetary terms, using these annual exemptions for one family, in any tax year, reduces the IHT bill by £1,200 immediately. For a couple, this is a saving of £2,400 a year. Over ten or twenty years the saving in tax adds up considerably. If you take into account all the exemptions, you can build a gradual but steady way of lowering the cost to your family in the full knowledge that doing so will have no undue effect on your lifestyle.

It is not widely known that people in certain 'risky' occupations are exempt from IHT if they die on active service. Included in this are armed forces personnel, police, firefighters, paramedics and humanitarian aid workers. This exemption also comes into play if a person was injured on active service and their death is hastened by the injury, even if they are no longer on active service when they die.

Charitable donations

You can also give any amount to charity while alive or in your will, which means that the donation will escape IHT, so you score on two points: saving tax and contributing positively to a charity or as many good causes as you wish. Moreover, if your church is a registered charity, there is income tax relief for higher-rate taxpayers on any covenants you make to it. Charities include museums, universities and some community amateur sports clubs (CASC). You will need to know the charity's registered name (its registered number will help, too) by checking the register in the country where you live.

You can donate:

- A fixed amount

- An item

- What you leave (eg in your will) after you have made other gifts

If you wish to give to several charities in your will, the Charities Aid Foundation (CAF) has a form you can complete with all the details, and they will ensure each charity gets their fair share on your death. Leaving gifts to charities in your will means you save IHT of 40% on each donation; moreover, you can reduce the IHT rate to 36% if you leave 10% or more of your estate to charity.[32]

Gift Aid

You can claim an extra 25p for every £1 you give, through Gift Aid. It will not cost you any extra. To do this, you must give a declaration to each charity to which you want to donate, through the Gift Aid scheme, but note:

- You can include all donations from the last four years; but, in any tax year, you need to pay enough income or capital gains tax to cover the extra 25% through Gift Aid.

- In other words, your donations will qualify if they are not more than four times what you paid in tax in that tax year (6 April to 5 April).

- You must tell the charities you support if you have not paid enough tax, or stop doing so.

- If you are a higher-rate taxpayer, you can claim the difference between the rate you pay and basic rate on your donation through your self-assessment return, if you complete one, or by informing HMRC. For example, let us assume you donate £500 to a charity. They claim Gift Aid, which makes your donation £625. You pay 40% tax, so you can claim back £125: £625 × (40% − 20%).

The donation need not be cash; it can be land or property. You will get income and capital gains tax relief (the income tax relief does not apply to gifts to CASCs). If the charity asks you to sell the asset on their behalf you can still get tax relief on any gains, but be sure to keep records of the gift and the charity's request.

Charities can claim Gift Aid on most donations, but payments do not qualify if they are:

- Made from limited companies

- Made through salary as payroll giving

- A payment for goods or services, or made because a charity or CASC has bought goods and services

- Originally loans, but no longer need to be repaid

- A source of 'benefit' to the donor, over a certain limit

- Made up of shares

- Charity cards or vouchers, such as CAF vouchers

- Membership fees to CASCs

- Received before the recipient became a charity or CASC

Foundations and trusts

You may wish to set up a family charitable foundation or trust. This too you can set up while still alive. You start by giving some of your assets to a trust or foundation, carrying a name you select, which is operated by your family and will continue after your death. A private family foundation is one way to create a framework which can establish a philanthropic legacy. It can also offer income tax and IHT benefits.

There is a bit more work than just making single donations to charity, so you may need some help. Again, the CAF is a useful resource. It is best to apply for charitable status with the Charity Commission, since without charitable status the trust will have to pay tax. However, this is straightforward to do. You will need to appoint trustees to manage the fund, who will probably include yourself and other members of the family. Foundations must contain a minimum of £20,000, but larger amounts are more cost-effective if you are running your own foundation. You will need to decide on which structure is right for you: a trust, a limited company, an unincorporated company or one limited by guarantee. Disadvantaged groups, promotion of education or medical knowledge and espousing religious principles should be acceptable, but political purposes may not be.

If you are doing it yourself, the assets need to be looked after, there are records to keep and research to carry out for your causes; the larger the endowment, the more work involved. You will need to draw up accounts each year, overseen by somebody competent. You and the other trustees will need to meet regularly to decide which causes you wish to help. There will need to be clear objectives and a plan of what you want to do and how you are going to go about it, which you should review from time to time. Creating a mission statement for your charity is a good way to start. If you have the time, knowledge and inclination then you may be quite happy to carry out these tasks. Alternatively, an accountant or solicitor can support you, and will charge fees.

I like the Charitable Aid Foundation. There are virtually no overheads, and you can dispense donations to charities already operational on the ground. Usually, you only need £10,000 to set up an arrangement with the CAF. This is effectively a bank account into which you make a single donation each year, and you can then use the account to make donations to charities. In addition, it makes your tax return easy, as you just record a single payment each year, and it does not involve administration and management work. You can set up a CAF account in your name, a family foundation's name, or choose to keep it anonymous.

A charitable trust can run indefinitely, particularly if your will adds a further gift to it. Just be sure that this is the right choice for you and your family, and that the groups or individuals you wish to benefit are already covered by other charities.

Allowances and reliefs

The various exemptions and charitable donations, if used regularly, will slowly chip away at any IHT. Allowances and reliefs will depend on your circumstances but are likely to lead to a much greater reduction of tax, provided you meet all the conditions. Usually, only larger estates – a business or a farm – will be able to benefit. There are some reliefs that do not even require these, such as investing in forestry.

Business Relief

Where you own shares controlling over 50% of the voting rights in a listed company, Business Relief

(BR) reduces the value of the company or its assets by 50% or 100%, which you can pass on while you are still alive or in your will. Your executors make the claim on your death, in assessing the value of your estate for probate. Included in a claim would be some or all:

- Property and buildings

- Unlisted shares

- Machinery

- Land, buildings, or machinery owned by you and used in a business in which you were a partner or held control

- Land, buildings, or machinery used in the business and held in a trust that the business may benefit from

These are the conditions for obtaining 100% relief:

- It must be an operating business or an interest in a business

- Or shares in an unlisted company

- You can only get relief if your death occurs at least two years after acquiring the business or asset

To avoid confusion, you cannot get BR if the company:

- Mainly deals with securities, stocks or shares, land or buildings, or in making or holding investments

- Is a not-for-profit organisation

- Is being sold, unless you are selling its shares to a company that will carry on the business and that company receives those shares

- Is being wound up, unless this is part of a process to allow the business of the company to carry on

Also, you cannot claim for additional reliefs if the business did not trade during the two years before it was passed on as a gift or in your will. Neither should they require such reliefs for future use in order to carry on the business. Where you use part of a nonqualifying asset in the business, that part might qualify for BR. For example, if you use one room in a building as a shop and the other rooms are residential, the shop will qualify for BR, but the rooms will not.

If you wish to give away all or part of your business while still alive, the estate can still get BR on IHT, if the property or assets qualify and if you owned the business or asset for at least two years before the date you gave or sold it. If you give away business property or assets, the recipient must keep them as a going concern if they want to keep the relief. They can, however, replace the property or assets – for example, machinery – with something of equal value if the replacement is for the business. Be prepared to pay capital gains tax or income tax if you sell, give away or dispose of an asset or property that has gone up in value during the time you owned it.

You do not actually have to have owned a business to qualify for this relief. As described in Chapter Two, 'Seven ways to mitigate inheritance tax', if you own shares in a company which has been trading for two years, you may claim 50% or 100% relief on your shareholding. We know these as Business Relief investments or 'BR'. Investing money in this way means that you get the reduction in tax after two years, which may help you if you are getting on in years and/or in ill health. You might feel uncertain about surviving a gift for seven years, so this can be a simple way round.

These types of schemes have operated for many years now, so several companies that promote them have gained a reputation and a track record. This is important, because the downside to BRs is that they usually invest in the AIM. Their value can fall and rise; AIM shares are typically far more volatile than those listed in the FTSE 250 or 100 Indexes, large, long-established companies. Often AIM shares are start-up companies or ones that have not yet got a good track record. Performance will rely on a good fund manager who can spot opportunities and then sell them quickly to make a profit. Unlike established companies, growth may not be that steady and dividends few in the earlier years.

Tax rules could change in the future, and the value of tax reliefs will depend on your personal circumstances. There is no guarantee that companies that qualify for BR today will continue to do so in the future.

Still, if you are not risk adverse, they could still be a useful part of your overall portfolio, offering a means of saving IHT, provided that the holding is in proportion to the risk you can tolerate and represents an amount that you can stand to lose.

Other means of obtaining Business Relief

Investing in forestry is also a means of obtaining BR. If the investment is structured in the right way, commercial forestry represents a shelter against IHT while also producing periodic tax-free income when mature trees are felled and the timber is sold. Forests must have been owned for five years.

If you own a stately home, land of outstanding natural beauty or objects of national scientific, historic or artistic importance (eg famous works of art), you could claim relief from IHT, subject to certain conditions.

The other important relief is one for farmers and owners of agricultural land, again during your lifetime or when passed on in your will. Agricultural property that qualifies for relief is land or pasture used to grow crops, to rear animals intensively or some other farming activities. The property must be part of a working farm in the UK. It must have been owned or occupied for agricultural purposes for two years if occupied by the owner, a company controlled by them, or their spouse or civil partner; or seven years if occupied by someone else (for example, let). It is important to be aware what does not qualify for agricultural relief (AR).

In the UK, habitat schemes were introduced to help to preserve the character of the countryside and maintain a habitat for wild animals and birds. These schemes ban agricultural production for long periods and land managed under these schemes would not normally qualify for AR.

If you originally inherited the property from someone other than a spouse or civil partner, HMRC calculates the period of ownership from that first death. There are various other conditions, particularly in relation to property and mortgages. If you are concerned about AR, then you should seek expert help from a lawyer.

CASE STUDY: AGRICULTURAL RELIEF

Deborah wants to 'downsize'. She owns a large farmhouse, which has a substantial amount of land attached to it. Her son has built his own house on part of the land, so this poses a problem if she does sell. She would like to sell the farm and live in a smaller property with local amenities, now that she is in her 70s. She tells me she does not want to be a burden on her son. Her problem is that she could well lose valuable agricultural relief.

A Furnished Holiday Let ('FHL') business may qualify as a business property for BR. However, this is an active area for case law.

Where assets qualify for BR or AR, you may gift them free of IHT. It might be preferable for your will to pass these assets to a trust instead of directly to the beneficiaries. This approach means that, instead of having mutual wills and each spouse leaving to the other, whichever spouse survives can continue to enjoy those assets without them passing into their estate for IHT. If the survivor then keeps the property that qualifies for BR or AR, then it is sometimes possible to double the relief. As always, you need specialist advice. The costs are more than likely to outweigh the benefits if a 'bespoke' scheme is drawn up to manage this.

Trusts

Setting up a trust can be part of your Family Wealth Plan, provided you are clear about its use, and it achieves your objectives.

Trusts can be straightforward or complex. They are often perceived as rigid, complicated, time-consuming and difficult to extract assets from. I feel that much of that has changed, provided you understand why you are using a trust, you use the right one and you realise its purpose. They have also been used to evade tax, but I am not espousing that.

A trust is a legal entity that holds property, cash or investments for the benefits of others. It will usually have a deed to set it up which establishes the rules by which it can operate: what the trustees can and cannot do with it. Trustees have specific duties laid down in the trusts you set up. Their job is to look after the assets of the trust and pay out income or capital to the beneficiaries named in it. They will have to manage the trust on a day-to-day basis, be responsible for any taxes and submit paperwork to HMRC. Again, the general duties of trustees you can find online.[33]

They will manage any savings and investments and keep them safe. Essentially, they must look after them as if it were their own money. If you appoint more than one trustee (as you should, unless you decide to appoint a firm of professional trustees), one of them will have to organise trustee meetings, act as chair, and keep minutes. This is a role that can last much longer than that of an attorney or executor. Some of the beneficiaries could be young children, or have health conditions or disabilities, and it might be years before the trust passes assets to them. The trust can pay trustees' expenses, but generally they will not be paid for their work unless the trust specifically provides for this (which it might if you appoint professional trustees).

A trustee can be a beneficiary (but this might be a bad idea, as it introduces an obvious conflict of interest).

The trustees can engage professionals such as financial advisers, investment managers, accountants or solicitors. But they must act personally, without conflicts of interest, and where there is more than one trustee, generally they must act unanimously, so ideally they must get along, and all will have to sign any paperwork.

Gifting into trust means that you can make much larger gifts at the same time as making use of the smaller exemptions and allowances. If the gift is bigger than the exemptions and allowances, then it is classed as a PET and you will need to survive it by seven years, before it falls outside your estate. Any gift (no matter the size) must be unconditional, or the Capital Taxes Office (CTO) will class it as a 'gift with reservation' (GWR) counting for IHT. Fortunately, from three years of making a gift there is taper relief on any IHT due. From year 4, this is 20% each year until year 7. So, if you find you have left a gift or transfer too late, or you become terminally ill, there is still a chance of saving some tax.

The person who gives assets to the trust is known as its 'settlor', and would often be a trustee, although this is unnecessary. You would also have other trustees (at least two or three, or a specialist trustee firm) who you hope will outlive you so they can administer it long after your death. All trustees should be familiar with their duties, as they are the legal owners of the assets in the fund. Addressing these issues is better while you are still alive. You can remove trustees and appoint others (or add trustees to the board), but both the departing and the arriving trustees must agree and usually a new trust deed will be needed to do this.

Complexity will depend on the assets invested in the trust. The more you have and the more types, the more likely it is tax returns will have to be completed. Records are necessary and trusts need to register with HMRC.

You can establish a trust with £10, and put no other assets in it until your death. Alternatively, you can add to it immediately or over time, providing the value of the gift is not over the NRB threshold for the first estate (currently £325,000: see Chapter Two) and if you survive the gift for seven years it will no longer form part of your estate when your executors calculate IHT. Timing of gifts into trust is important and the order in which you make these gifts can affect the amount of IHT ultimately charged.

If setting up the trust to mitigate tax, you must not receive any benefit from the assets; so you cannot draw the income from a rental property, for example. There are trusts that allow you, the settlor, to keep an interest and therefore benefit, but their purpose is different, and they will not help you cascade wealth and save IHT.

These are the main types of trust.

Bare trusts

Here the beneficiary has the right to all the capital in, and the income from, the trust once they are 18 or over (in England and Wales), or 16 or over (in Scotland). This means the assets set aside by the settlor will always go directly to the intended beneficiary. They are often used to pass assets to young people – the trustees look after them until the beneficiary is old enough.

Interest-in-possession trusts

Under these trusts the trustee must pass on all trust income to the beneficiary as it arises (less any expenses). Since 2008, beneficiaries of such a trust cannot transfer this income. A tax charge will be payable unless it is a disabled trust.

EXAMPLE: INTEREST-IN-POSSESSION

You create a trust and transfer to it all the shares you own. The terms say that, after you die, the income from those shares will go to your spouse for the rest of their life. When they die, the shares will pass to your children.

Your spouse does not have a right to the shares. (If the trust holds a property, they become a life tenant. They can live in the property for their lifetime, but they do not own it.)

If you inherit an interest-in-possession trust from someone who has died, there is no IHT at the ten-year anniversary (described below). Instead, 40% tax will be due when you die.

Discretionary trusts

These types of trust are popular because of their flexibility: they allow the trustees to make decisions about how to use the trust income, and sometimes the capital, as specified in the trust deed, which gives them guidance on what to pay out (income or capital), to whom and how.

You might set up a discretionary trust to put assets aside for:

- A future need, such as a grandchild who may need more financial help than other beneficiaries

- Children whose parents have died

- Beneficiaries who are not capable or responsible enough to deal with money themselves

Accumulation trusts

Under this type, the trustees accumulate income within the trust and add it to the trust's capital. They may also pay income out, and may have discretion over when and how to do so.

Mixed trusts

These are a combination of different types of trust. There can be special tax treatment for mixed trusts, including IHT treatment.

Tax on trusts

Trusts are usually subject to phased IHT charges every ten years, known as the 'periodic' charge, but trusts with vulnerable beneficiaries are exempt.

There are different rates of income tax for any income or dividends, so it pays to seek professional advice before establishing a trust and adding assets to it, especially as who pays the tax can vary depending on the type of trust. Likewise, putting assets into a trust or indeed taking them out or selling them, may trigger a capital gain on which tax will be due. The allowance for capital gains in a trust is half the allowance for an individual.

You can write your will so that a trust does not come into effect until you die; this is known as a 'will trust'. It was a popular way of using two NRBs before 2007, when the law changed to allow a spouse to pass on their allowance to a surviving spouse. However, it can avoid 'sideways disinheritance'. This occurs when the first partner dies, leaving children from the marriage who might reasonably expect to inherit part of the family estate in due course. If the surviving partner remarries and cannot make provision for their children in a new will, there is a risk that everything will go to the new spouse instead. To avoid this, you could set up a life interest trust in your will, which leaves your share of the family home to your children, while allowing your spouse to carry on enjoying the right to live in the property.

Establishing trusts could give you an element of control you would not have if you gave assets outright. If this is what you are seeking to achieve with your Family Wealth Plan, then trusts may be the right vehicle for you. There can also be tax advantages, but that should never be the main reason for setting one up. Assets in trust are not part of your estate so not subject to probate and some of those funds may be useful in paying bills until probate is obtained.

As with most of the advice in this book, you should seek expert help from your Financial Planner, adviser or solicitor on what any of what I describe might mean in your circumstances.

Summary

Making use of the exemptions and smaller allowances under IHT, and charitable donations, will help cascade your wealth and your Family Wealth Plan should set out what you decide. Trusts can be a useful tool in a few ways, not just to save tax. While protecting assets, they can also safeguard those for the young and vulnerable. Trusts can help you plan retirement, make gifts to charity, provide for descendants' education, buy a home for your children, or protect assets in marriage and from divorce, death or disability of anyone involved.

Keeping excellent records for your executors is a must. Otherwise, you could lose the whole point of making the gifts or donations, and fail to save tax.

You need to assess whether any of these ways to mitigate IHT are right for you and your family. Your Family Wealth Plan will help you decide the most appropriate approach. Making use of trusts most definitely requires specialist advice. As a trust is a legal document, there must be care in establishing them. A minor error or omission could cause it to unravel. An expert will ensure that they are in order. Otherwise, your family may rue the day you made this decision, rather than appreciate your judicious choice of instrument in saving them tax or protecting your wealth.

PART THREE
Cascading Your Wealth

You should by now be in an excellent position to decide on how to develop your Family Wealth Plan. Cascading your wealth is now a matter of putting some of these decisions into action. Paperwork and various legal documents will be necessary, as the plan will not work without them. There is no reason you cannot set up some of these yourself but, after reading the next chapter, I hope you will see the advantages of professional help and guidance.

SIX

T Is About Taking Action

This chapter examines the documents necessary to put your Family Wealth Plan into action. Without them, you have only gone so far. Step 5 in the implementation of the plan brings it all together. If your planner or adviser liaises with other professionals and those with responsibilities for carrying out the actions now or in due course, even better. They can ensure that everyone is acting together on your behalf and understands what you are trying to achieve. They can also ensure that they put the plan into action with each person carrying out their part. Your planner, who has an overall review of your plan, can report back to you on progress. This person can make sure that you get it all in order.

Powers of Attorney

Someone once said to me that setting up a Power of Attorney (POA) for her mother was the best piece of advice I had ever given her. She told me it saved her so much hassle and she could sort out her mother's affairs far more easily once it was in place.

While you may think either that you will not need such an instrument or that the need for it is a long way off, it will probably be too late if you lose capacity, suddenly have a stroke, suffer paralysis or develop dementia. These are all morbid subjects, I know, that you may not wish to think about, but if you are serious about putting your affairs in order, Powers of Attorney are essential, and the sooner you get them completed and registered, the better.

You may have seen or read about Kate Garraway, the TV presenter, and her husband, who was ill with COVID-19 for more than a year. Much of that time, he was in a coma. Having her husband seriously ill for so long was bad enough, but she could not access his bank or credit card accounts or refinance the mortgage.

She did not even have the legal right to view his medical notes under data protection laws. She could have avoided all this had they put Lasting Powers of Attorney in place.

Now, you may already have sorted out Powers of Attorney years ago, and if that is the case, it is probably an Enduring Power of Attorney (EPA). These only required one person to act as the attorney and they did not have to be registered immediately. In fact, if you still have full mental capacity, your attorney can still use it on your behalf. EPAs only cover financial decisions and can be useful for temporary decisions or ones that need to be made quickly.

However, if you were diagnosed with dementia, for example, your EPA would have to be registered, and valuable time would be lost waiting for the Office of the Public Guardian (OPG) to complete registration on your behalf. Still, it was a quick and relatively cheap way of establishing a Power of Attorney. The OPG checks and registers all Powers of Attorney and there are useful helplines and information if you need help.[34]

The Mental Capacity Act 2005 came into effect on 1 October 2007, and under it Lasting Powers of Attorney (LPAs) replaced EPAs. The purpose was to prevent exploitation and abuse of someone in a vulnerable position, as there had been several incidences of this. A minimum of two attorneys must be in place, to decide on behalf of another person. Now, there are two types of LPA: one covers property and financial matters (as EPAs did); the other covers health and welfare. It is best to set up both, even though you may consider the health and welfare power not that crucial.

Therefore, think of those to whom you give this duty. I described different roles and responsibilities that people must carry in Chapter Four. When your attorneys must act on your behalf, you might not be in any condition to be consulted. They will have to decide on your behalf.

CASE STUDY: AUTHORITY TO CUT OFF LIFE SUPPORT

Edith's dementia had become so bad that she was not eating or drinking liquids; she was in hospital and put on a glucose feed. However, after a while, the consultant suggested end-of-life care.

Her son, Mark, knew it was the right thing to do, having watched Edith's quality of life fade away over the weeks. The hospital was just keeping a corpse alive. However, he felt terrible giving the approval that was needed, as if he were ordering the death of his own mother. He could not discuss it with her, clearly. Had a health and welfare LPA been in place, with a clear declaration from Edith about life support, it would have made that decision so much easier for Mark to bear.

Setting up an LPA while you are fit and well, you can be clear about your wants and needs. If you lose mental capacity, you lose the right to establish one, and it cannot be done for you without going to court, just as you can only give instructions for a will while you are of sound mind.

You cannot use LPA unless you register them: they have no legal force until you do. If you do not arrange this, then your attorneys can, but you can lose time this way. You can appoint more than two people, but unlike trustees they can act jointly or severally. Will you be sure what is the best for you? If you select friends or family as your attorneys, you need to make sure they can act in harmony over your affairs.

Would you know whether you need replacement attorneys and for what reason? Do you want one pair of attorneys for one LPA and a different pair for the other? You can give detailed descriptions about what your attorneys can and cannot do, even permit them to act on your behalf while you still have capacity. You can instruct who should manage your investments, or how you wish them to be managed and which professionals they should use. This is important if you want continuity as, if the LPA lacks this instruction, the management of your portfolio, especially if discretionary, may stop as soon as the Power of Attorney starts to be used.

Also, where do you want to spend your last days and weeks if you become terminally ill: at home, in a hospice or hospital? You can prescribe all this in LPAs, but it would be useful to talk this through with an adviser or solicitor.

You can set up a power on your own, online, and while it is much cheaper and seems straightforward,

I would caution against this. I am not sure you will always get the best result for you. There must be clarity about how the attorneys will act. Unforeseen circumstances could arise, that would cost you more in the long run. As usual, speak to someone who can give you expert advice.

Once established and registered, you can keep LPAs with your personal papers, certify a couple of copies for your attorneys to keep or pay to keep them in storage until needed. If a solicitor has drawn these up for you, they will certify them for you. However, you must sign every page, and the last page, twice. When it comes to looking after your finances and property, your health and your welfare, who better to decide what you require and what is most suitable, than yourself?

Provided you still have capacity, you can ask the OPG to change an LPA if you have registered it. If you want to remove an attorney, you will need to send OPG a written statement called a partial deed of revocation. You must write to OPG if one of your attorneys changes their name – by marriage or deed poll or address – and provide supporting documents. If one of your attorneys dies, you must tell OPG and send them a copy of the death certificate, the original LPA and all certified copies. This can be time-consuming and tedious, but fortunately the OPG has introduced a new online service to overcome this. You can create an account online and use the activation key to add LPAs to your account.

This will improve the speed with which attorneys can make important decisions, such as those related to their loved ones' care or property. The new system will allow those acting as an attorney to provide a secure code, which when submitted to the online portal will nearly instantaneously confirm their status as an attorney and the power they hold – authorising them to take actions on your behalf. The new system, known as 'Use a Lasting Power of Attorney', has been available since 17 July 2020 for newly registered LPAs, but the OPG is working on extending this system to LPAs already registered. It saves on the need for certified copies to take to banks and other institutions.

There must be a will

Writing a will is essential. It is surprising how many people do not write one, even some of the richest and best-known. Both Prince and Aretha Franklin died intestate, for example.

If you do not have a will, intestacy rules may cover your estate. Depending on the size of your family and the number in the next generations, they may deal adequately with what you leave. But if you have a fair amount of wealth and are concerned about how to pass it on, perhaps now, but mainly after your death, there are no ifs, ands, or buts: a will is crucial. And if you and your partner separate, divorce or one of you dies, then you should make a new will. If you lose one of your potential beneficiaries or change your mind about something, then you can add a codicil.

Marrying, remarrying or entering a civil partnership cancels an existing will. Divorce does not automatically invalidate a will but excludes your ex-spouse (ex-civil partner) from benefiting if you described them in your will as 'my spouse' ('my civil partner').

A will is essential if you are not married or have remarried and you want to ensure that your first offspring benefit rather than (or as well as) those of your new spouse or partner. Making use of trust in your will can safeguard the positions of people in a range of relationships. Intestacy rules do not recognise an unmarried partner, no matter how long you have been living together or whether there are children from that relationship, although your children will have rights.

If you have young children, then you may need to appoint guardians until they attain the age of 18. If so, you need to get permission from the people you choose. They must be happy to care for and bring up your children, and look after any funds left to them (which will usually be placed in trust for the guardians/trustees to use on the children's behalf). Under the Children's Act 1989, guardians have the legal right to take care of the child and to make important decisions in their life. If both you and your partner have parental responsibility, the guardianship will not take effect until both parents have died. If you do not appoint a guardian in your will, the courts may appoint someone for you. This may not be the person you would prefer to look after your child on your death.

Of course, you can buy DIY wills at well-known stationers or online, but unless you are in the legal profession, do not even consider this. Solicitors say they make much more money on disputes over badly put-together wills than on drawing up a will properly. The last thing you want is your family to dispute over your will or, worse still, to launch an expensive court battle over your hard-earned cash and possessions.

No matter how thorough your will is, you may forget to account for part of your estate. Your will should include a 'residuary gift' clause that sets out who will inherit anything not otherwise given away in the will. Such a clause should also state what would happen if one of your beneficiaries should die before you. If there is no residuary gift clause, the executors must divide up the part not accounted for under the laws of intestacy.

Apart from being clear in your will about your wishes and who you want to execute it, you can also add a letter of wishes. Instead of sometimes-confusing legalese, you can write this in your own words, so that your descendants know that the will is what you intended. Such a letter to (say) your family could say things like 'I leave you to decide on my personal possessions such as my art or stamp collection, but ask you not to fight over them and share them out fairly and amicably'. This might not prevent disputes altogether, but it could make the division of the spoils more sensible, or head off claims that your will was not what you actually wished.

You do not have to tell any family or friends what your will states if you do not want to, but it could help beneficiaries to know roughly what to expect, or that they can expect an inheritance.

For a will to be valid:

- It must be in writing, signed and witnessed (see next section).

- At the time you sign it, you must have the mental capacity to make the will and understand the effect it will have.

- You must have made the will voluntarily and without pressure from anyone else.

The beginning of the will should state that it revokes all others. If you made an earlier will, destroy it unless you have property overseas – the revocation will not cover a foreign will. If you have property abroad, then you should consider an offshore or international will. Getting expert advice in this area will be in your best interests as it will help with different countries' inheritance rules. There are lawyers in the UK who can give this advice.

Signing a will

You must sign your will watched by two independent witnesses over the age of 18, who must also sign it in your presence – so all three people should be in the room together when each one signs. If anyone signs the will incorrectly, it is not valid. Do not feel you need to choose family members or partners, boyfriends or girlfriends of family – this might even be a mistake if (say) you are not planning to leave them what they might expect. The witnesses do not have to know you or even read the will; they just act as witnesses.

When you cannot make a will

If you have lost mental capacity,[35] you cannot make a will. Even a serious illness or a diagnosis (of dementia, say) could prevent you from making a will and it is your professional adviser's job to ensure that you can make these decisions. Someone can sign a will drawn up on your behalf provided you are in the room, and you have capacity at that moment. You may need a medical practitioner's statement at the time the will is signed, certifying that you understand what you are signing.

Therefore, there should be no possibility of your actions being questioned. Acrimony can really kick off when a parent dies if the family does not see the will as even-handed. During a time of considerable distress, they may perceive money as a sign of parental affection, and any anger can quickly spill into feuds and legal challenges. The President of the Law Society, who has reported on the matter, reinforces this view:

> Writing a legally valid will with the help of an expert solicitor ensures people's estates are inherited exactly as they would choose and can prevent a whole raft of problems landing on loved ones when they are grieving.[36]

Rules of intestacy and living wills

The rules of intestacy provide for beneficiaries in the following hierarchy, with no provision made for stepchildren of the deceased:

- Your spouse or civil partner, who inherit all your personal possessions and
- At least the first £270,000 of your estate, plus half the rest
- If you have no children, your entire estate
- Your children (blood or adopted), if you leave no spouse or civil partner (ie in these circumstances they will inherit everything, divided equally between them)
- Your parents

- Your siblings (full siblings coming before half siblings)

- Your grandparents

- Your aunts and uncles

- Your cousins

- If you leave no living relatives, the Crown

If you are not married or in a civil partnership and have not made a will, there is no automatic right to inherit from your estate, even where you leave a partner, no matter how long you have lived together and whether you have children. If you do not have a partner or children, then your estate will be passed on in the above order, starting from the point in the hierarchy that applies in your case.

If you wish stepchildren, an unmarried partner, children from that relationship or other people not listed above to inherit from you, make a will that includes them.

How a stepchild can make a claim

There is only one option available to stepchildren where either they have been left out of a will, or their stepparent has died intestate, which is to bring a claim under the Inheritance (Provision for Family and Dependants) Act 1975. To succeed under the act, a stepchild must be able to show two things:

1. They must have been treated as a child of the family by a married stepparent or financially depended on the stepparent.

2. The stepparent made no provision, or inadequate provision, for them in a will (or left no will).

Whether a claim is likely to succeed will depend upon:

- The age of the stepchild

- The size of the estate

- The financial needs of any other beneficiaries or claimants

- The needs of the stepchild, including any special needs

- Any future needs of the stepchild

- The stepchild's degree of dependency on the stepparent

A claim under the Inheritance (Provision for Family and Dependants) Act 1975 must be brought within six months of probate being granted, so time will be very much of the essence.

Same-sex couples

If you are in a same-sex relationship, you may well be thinking about entering a civil partnership or marriage. That would treat the two of you as each other's spouses under the intestacy rules. If either or both of you have children for whom you have parental responsibility, you would each gain parental responsibility for the other's children. However, that does not mean that your newly recognised stepchildren would inherit under the intestacy rules (see above). It simply places you in the same position as a married couple with stepchildren.

In 2017, the Office for National Statistics (ONS) recorded the numbers of same-sex couples in the following three categories:[37]

1. Same-sex married couples – 34,000

2. Civil partnership couples – 55,000

3. Same-sex cohabiting couples – 101,000

As you can see, the number of same-sex couples cohabiting is far larger than those either married or in a civil partnership. This means that a substantial number of same-sex couples currently have little legal recognition of their relationship.

Living wills

In the UK, we legally recognise the term 'living will'. It is an 'advance decision', 'advance statement' or 'advance directive'.

This is a document outlining your wishes regarding healthcare and medical treatments if you cannot communicate this information yourself. Unlike an LPA for health and welfare, under which you hand over responsibility, these benefit those who want to make their wishes known themselves (not through an agent) and who:

- Have chronic health issues

- Have been diagnosed with a life-threatening or terminal illness

- Are reaching old age

- Are preparing for travel

- Are preparing for an event that could cause injury (such as a marathon or skydive)

An 'advance decision to refuse treatment' lets you explain the medical treatment(s) you will not want doctors to give you if a time comes when you lack capacity and cannot make or communicate your wishes. You must express this while you still can make these decisions.

An 'advance statement' allows you to make general statements, describing your wishes and preferences about your future care if you cannot make or communicate a decision or express your preferences. There is no restriction on what you can express, and it does not have to be directed at medical staff. The statement can describe your preferences for palliative care, the music that you like to listen to, the clothes that you wish to wear and/or the visits you would like to receive and from whom. It is not legally binding. You are just documenting these preferences for the benefit of your family, who would hopefully respect your wishes. It is a useful document if you have named a Lasting Power of Attorney for health and welfare. This person will refer to your advance statement to guide their decisions.

A 'living will' ensures that your wishes will be clearly articulated and followed, even if you cannot express them, and provides medical professionals and your family with clear guidance. This can help prevent arguments about your care and reduce the cost of it if you choose to forgo life support. It speaks for you while you are alive and therefore you cannot include it in your will, which gives instructions for after you die.

If you have powerful feelings about your medical care, from a religious conviction or from seeing somebody else go through a traumatic experience, then you should seriously consider preparing an advance statement.

Accounting for it all

There is more to estate planning than simply writing a will. You can make life easier for those who survive you by accounting for all your assets. This, along with your wishes, will ensure your plan can be executed smoothly. Keeping a list of all your assets will help any executor(s) to distribute your estate among the people named in your will. As part of implementing your Family Wealth Plan, make lists, an inventory of all you own. Here is a useful checklist:

1. **Itemise personal possessions.** Look around your home, both inside and outside, and make a list of all valuable items. Examples include the home itself, television sets, jewellery, collectibles, vehicles, art and antiques, computers or laptops and power tools. The list will probably be much longer than you may have expected. As you continue, add notes if someone comes to mind who you would like to have the item after your death.

   My husband loves watches and has a small collection, which are not only valuable but quite covetable. I would not want to inherit them and have them sit in a drawer, but would rather they go to someone in the family who would really appreciate and use them. As the advert for Patek Philippe watches states, 'You never actually own a Patek Philippe. You merely look after it for the next generation.' (By the way, my husband does not own a Patek Philippe, but he would like to.)

   Likewise, the photographic equipment he has bought over the years he would readily give to his youngest daughter, who has inherited his love of and skill at photography. Any other member of the family might not value them so much. Conversely, his music collection, which is now mostly digital, holds many memories which the family will love to recall.

My daughter has already stated that she wants my handbag collection, whatever happens.

2. **Nonphysical assets.** Next, start adding your intangible assets to your list, such as things you own on paper, especially assets that would only activate on death. I mean here things like life insurance policies, bank and savings accounts, disability and health policies (including any for long-term care), household insurance and any policies on vehicles, motorbikes and bicycles. Might any certificates be necessary to prove ownership, cover or validity / value?

Include all the account numbers and list the location of the physical documents you hold. You may also want to list contact information for any firms holding these possessions.

3. **Memberships.** If you belong to any organisations, make a list of them. It would be helpful for those in charge to stop any mailings or other forms of contact. Include any charitable organisations that you support. This information may help your beneficiaries know which charities or causes are close to your heart and to which you might like donations to go in your memory.

4. **Any debts or liabilities?** Then make a separate list of credit cards and other commitments you may have. This should include items such as loans, mortgages, equity release and any other debts you owe. Again, add account numbers, the location of signed agreements and contact information for the companies holding the debt. Include all your credit cards, noting which ones you use regularly, and which ones sit in a drawer unused.

   Sometimes, it may be useful to run a free credit report from time to time. This will also identify any credit cards you might have forgotten about.

5. **Make copies.** When you have completed your lists, date and sign them and make at least three or four copies. Keep the originals with your personal documents such as your will, hopefully in storage. Leave a copy for your partner in a safe place. A third copy you might give to your Financial Planner, who will have all the details about your investments, plans and bank accounts. Keep the last copy for yourself, in a safe place that is different from where you keep the top copy.

Dealing with bank accounts on death

Assets bequeathed in a will usually need to go through probate, and the same is true when someone dies intestate. This process can be time-consuming.

However, many accounts, such as bank savings, although they form part of your estate can be used by your executors to cover any outstanding debts and taxes. In order to start this process, the bank may require a 'grant of representation' before releasing the funds. This is a catch-all term covering more specific documents, including the eventual grant of probate. If your executors can obtain a grant of representation, this confirms that they can legally take care of your estate and financial affairs.

The executors' responsibilities will include notifying your bank(s) of your death and providing them with a copy of the death certificate and some proof of their own identity. Once this is received, the bank will either freeze your account or close it fully – any direct debits or standing orders will be cancelled and any continuous payments stopped. Some banks may release the money immediately probate has been granted – each bank has its own threshold, and these can be between £15,000 and £50,000. However, most will want to see the grant document first, even if there is little money in the account.

While you are waiting for the probate to be granted, many banks allow executors to use the money in your account to pay expenses relating to the death – these can include:

- Organising and paying for a funeral
- Buying a headstone

- Paying any IHT (the tax needs to be paid before probate is granted)

- Paying probate fees

The bottom line

Procrastination is the biggest enemy of any planning, but especially estate planning. While none of us likes to think about our death, lack of proper, careful planning can lead to family disputes, assets being put in the wrong hands, long court litigation and excess money being paid in inheritance or other taxes. Benjamin Franklin once said, 'By failing to prepare, you are preparing to fail' – so pick a time and get started.

Summary

People often leave the drafting of these documents too late, or worse, do not do it at all. You cannot ignore the fact that this paperwork is an essential part of your Family Wealth Plan.

Choose your attorneys and executors well. They will carry immense responsibilities on your behalf.

As you now know, it is up to you what you give away in your will, how you divide it up and who or what you give it to (charities, sports clubs, cats' homes, etc). A will is the only way to make sure your money, property, possessions and investments (your estate) go to the people and causes you care about.

SEVEN

Staying On Track

So far, I have provided you with a wealth of information, tips, and advice on how to cascade your wealth. In reaching this stage, you can now put together your Family Wealth Plan using this knowledge. You will have determined what you want to achieve, have some ideas of what advice you like and what you do not. You will know for certain what you own and what you need, who is important to you and why. This chapter is all about putting it together to make sense of it. It will give you a path to follow. This will make sure you leave the legacy you wish to be remembered by.

Putting your Family Wealth Plan together

Getting all the information you need to make sense of what you own can be a painstaking and time-consuming exercise. Contacting all the providers, requesting current valuations and all the details possible on the plans, policies and investments you have is one part. In addition, it will pay to have land and property valued, and be aware of any inheritances you or your partner might receive. As fast as you gain details or values on one investment or plan, it can be out of date, because one or two of the providers are slow in delivering the information. To add to this frustration, you might find that some companies you have used are so long-standing that they have changed hands a few times and tracking them down consumes more of your time.

Then you will need to know exactly how much income you receive before tax. Tax calculations will give you your spendable income, and make sure you include everything such as interest and dividends. Do you get tax relief on charitable donations, pension contributions and covenants? Are you drawing down on your personal pension and if so, how long is it likely to last and is it all taxable? Do you receive other allowances? Do any have valuable guarantees and are any investments or life policies already in trust? What steps have you already taken, if any, to mitigate income, capital gains and inheritance tax? What kind of growth rates can you realistically expect on your investments?

Answers to these and many more questions are necessary to complete your Wealth Plan. The most important detail required is the cost of your lifestyle. Do not ask an adviser to tell you how much that might be, as everybody's standard of living is unique to them. It is essential that you try to account for every bit of spending for your life well-lived. To truly know how much is enough you would need to calculate all your outgoings. Some people find this an arduous task, but others keep spreadsheets or have excellent knowledge of their expenditure. One client kept a list of more expensive items in a notebook and could tell me how much he had paid for a jacket in 1989. I do not think you need to go that far, but it is worth keeping a note of major or variable expenditure.

Getting this right is crucial, since working out how much you need to maintain your desired standard of living is the foremost matter to be considered. By collating all the details of your assets, income and expenditure, we can assess any shortfalls or excesses in your financial future. It is likely that, if you have the riches that will attract IHT on your death, there may be no cash shortfalls, but this does not always follow, particularly if you have assets such as land or property which do not produce income.

Once you see the overall picture of your wealth, your spending habits, how long you need to rely on some of your capital, you can then consider your choices. Some of these I have already addressed.

Initially, you will need to work out whether you can enjoy your desired lifestyle throughout your lifetime. A good Financial Planner will produce some projections, perhaps up to your 100th birthday or even beyond, which is a worthwhile task. You gain reassurance once you know for sure how much you and a surviving partner need. Once you have worked out how much you need to keep for care costs, other contingencies and major expenditure, you can proceed to the next stage. This will be to prioritise the options you have selected. There will be some critical steps to take and paperwork to complete.

By now, you should have worked out what is important to you: whether to mitigate as much IHT as you can, or ignore it, will be part of this. Some I have discussed this with feel that paying tax is beneficial to the economy, or that after tax the family would still have plenty to share. Usually, though, parents are keen to pass on their wealth tax free. If you want to help your children and see them enjoy the gifts you make now while you are still living, then act on that decision. If you worry about overindulging them, then either make time to talk to them or put gifts into trust and let them know that the money is available if they need it for future development, education or buying a property, as and when they really need it.

There is no right or wrong about this; it must be what is right for you and your partner (if you have one). It is worth taking some time to reflect on these questions, as otherwise your Family Wealth Plan will not really achieve all that you want it to. This Analysis and subsequent strategy help to build the Plan, help you own and identify with it, and be happy to update regularly. This will be vital to its success. It is a living, moving object because your circumstances will change, as will those of other family members. Over time, legislation, taxation, inflation, interest rates, stock market performance and the economy will all change.

You cannot put it in a drawer and forget about it, because if you do all your efforts will have been a waste of time. Apart from that, the plan will give you reassurance about your destiny and that of any partner. It will be there as a reference point in any eventuality, especially in the event of long-term incapacity or death. You will have a wonderful knowledge of what you can and cannot afford to do. You will know how much (if any) of your estate will have to be paid in taxes. If cascading your wealth is your aim, this will encourage you to follow your plan to act on it.

Preserving family wealth requires careful planning. Just as a business carries out strategic planning to help reach its goals, a family needs to plan the steps to building family wealth. It is difficult to reach goals without a plan.

Decisions, decisions

The Family Wealth Plan will show you where you are now: what you own, what it is worth and what you can and cannot do with it. All the costs are clear, and you should now have comparisons with existing plans alongside future recommendations. You can compare what your circumstances would be if you do nothing with what they would be if you decide to make any of the changes. It will show how much tax you will save, and what your beneficiaries can and cannot expect to happen. Most important, it will give you the opportunity to put your house in order, tidy up loose ends and ensure you have all the right paperwork and documents in place. Kept with your personal papers for your family to read, your Family Wealth Plan adds to any instructions you have left and can give them a better understanding of your objectives.

I recall one family having a Bible in which they wrote down all important events and every member of the family. It was more than a family tree, though these can be useful: it added helpful descriptions about various personalities and their intentions.

Once you have all the information at your fingertips and know that your lifestyle and that of a partner is secure, no matter what happens, this will enable you to make choices and finally, decisions. One aspect which I have already covered is whether you give to the next generation now or on your death. If you are happy to be the 'bank of mum and dad', make those gifts special, if you can. Giving on a birthday or a special celebration, when they least expect it, will make their day, if not their year.

CASE STUDY: HOW GIFTS CAN HELP NOW

Roger told me that, after he had given his goddaughter £250,000 at Christmas, she began to send him text messages filled with heart emojis and kisses. She was obviously showing her delight and gratitude, but those little symbols added to his enjoyment of the gift. It is one thing to give; it is another to have the gift really appreciated. That sum of money helped her to buy a house and I am sure made a big difference to her life. It was also totally unexpected.

Clearly, Roger had to work out first whether it would be tax-efficient to make the gift, and he knows that he must survive it for seven years to avoid any IHT.

Once you have made your decisions, carry them through, as not only will you have had to spend valuable time to get to that point, but money too. Go through the plan diligently, note down questions or queries you may have. Be sure to get answers that are clear and satisfy you. You might include a timeline, perhaps for tax timing or maturity of products that you cannot draw on straight away, so will need to keep you on track (or need help managing).

If you have life cover that needs to be put in trust, then deal with the paperwork, get it all witnessed. Once you have decided who will be your executors, trustees and attorneys, talk to them and give them the information they need. To help them with their decisions, you can ask them to read the relevant chapter of this book. If they are still prepared to take on the tasks, then you have more reassurance that they will act in your best interests. They will act on your wishes and ensure that your beneficiaries receive their inheritance. There should be little confusion or lack of awareness when the time comes to act.

Be sure about the division of the estate, what charities you wish to include and any special bequests (such as my husband's collections). Even if not valuable, someone in the family may feel sentimental attachments to something, and may hope for possession. For me, it would be my art collection: there is no point leaving it to people who do not appreciate modern art or even like what they see. Since Richard, my husband, is an amateur photographer, we have albums of photographs, slides, and videos and digital copies. Our grandchildren (all under the age of 10) love looking through them now; but in years to come how fascinated would they be to look back on these collections and possibly share them with their own children?

Protecting your wealth is all part of the process and you will need a good wealth manager to help you look after your investments. You need sound active management of them while keeping costs reasonable. You want them to remain in line with the level of risk you are prepared to take, which might require the funds to be rebalanced and compared with agreed benchmarks. Too many people put their money in funds, rarely look at them then complain, when they finally do, that the performance has been poor.

Make sure you have copies of every crucial document, especially trust deeds, wills, and Powers of Attorney, and keep these in one place. You can let important people (your partner, attorneys or executors) know where you keep them. The originals you can keep in storage, but again leave information where these are stored. The important people will need to know who they should contact and who your important advisers are. Keep information on their addresses, contact numbers, etc, especially changes of names and/or addresses of your central group, who will have duties to perform.

You may have to put in place some new life cover, which could also require trust wrappers. If you have properties which you rent, maybe you could transfer these to a limited liability company or hold them in a Self-invested Personal Pension (SIPP)? Any capital gains or Stamp Duty Land Tax (SDLT) would need to be calculated. Transferring any assets into trusts, a limited company or even directly to someone may incur tax. There is much to consider, but you must do this.

For many of you, this process will involve accountants and solicitors, and someone needs to liaise with them to put your wealth plan in place. They may have ideas of improvements that you can make, so if you have professional advisers in mind, be sure to connect them early on.

Whatever you decide, you and your family now have sufficient knowledge and greater security that you will achieve what you have set out to do. There will be no doubts about the future, no shocks or surprises that you have not prepared for.

Keeping control

Even if you do not gift your estate during your lifetime, it is important to maintain control of your plans and actions. Just because you have put your house in order and implemented all the important matters, does not mean there is nothing more to be done. Just as you and a partner's or even family members' circumstances change, so can the assets you own.

Ageing, poor health, deaths, births and marriages can occur in a family, and all will have their effect. Each separation or divorce can affect your plans. Some may inherit from other family members or friends, sell businesses, face unemployment, even emigrate. Family members may become estranged because of disputes. The list is endless.

Therefore, it is essential to review your Family Wealth Plan at least once a year with the professionals you use. By now, they will have got to know you and your family well, and the values you espouse. They will understand your purpose, vision and mission in life and where you are heading. You can easily update the Family Wealth Plan with new values and fresh calculations (if needed). Are you still on track, do you still have enough to maintain your desired lifestyle now and in any circumstance?

This reassessment of your planning may prompt some modifications, possibly to your will, perhaps through adding a codicil. If in the intervening period significant changes affect various people who were to play a role in your estate planning, do you need to amend other documents such as Powers of Attorney, or your beneficiaries, executors or trustees?

Changes such as these, or even changing your own mind, might lead you to gift now rather than later. Some people do this if they decide to downsize and raise cash from the equity in a home that they no longer need. The beauty of working with many members of one family, as I often do, is that some decisions the different parties can make are especially satisfying.

CASE STUDY: LIFETIME GIFTING

Take David, who was fast approaching 90, and Heather, in her mid-80s, a married couple I had known for several years. They were independent people and mostly in good health, but their mobility was shrinking: they found it difficult to drive a couple of miles to the shops. This led them to sell a large semi for a smaller place in the middle of town with immediate access to all the facilities. Friends and family thought they were making a big mistake. 'They would miss the garden', said one. 'They won't like a smaller kitchen', said another.

I discovered that neither of these mattered at all; quality of life was paramount and they wanted to preserve this. I urged them not to be concerned about what others might say, even though those others meant well.

They had hardly touched their investment portfolio in all the time I had known them. So, when they asked me what they should with the money they now held after downsizing, I did not hesitate in suggesting they give it to their two children, Harry and Fiona. Harry wanted to build an extension on his home, and it was clearly going to cost. I knew that Fiona's businesses had been facing difficulties, while their children were still at university.

The benefit to David and Heather was witnessing the surprised delight of their children and what a difference this money made to their lives. Of course, David and Heather had a Family Wealth Plan, so knew that, despite this generous gift, their financial future was secure, and they would have no need of the money themselves. They are happy to be in their new home, too, and settled there well.

They have documented the two gifts and hope they will survive them for seven years, saving their children 40% in IHT; and in any case the taper relief will begin after three years (see Chapter Five). Had the couple left the money in their estate, no doubt it would have grown, and the ultimate tax bill with it. The children would have appreciated their legacy, but certainly not as much as while David and Heather were still alive.

This is not the first time I have suggested gifting excess capital to your children during your lifetime, and it probably will not be the last. Parents often do not have this idea themselves, although many readily agree once it is suggested.

Staying on track and staying in control are all part of the process of the Family Wealth Plan. There is no point in going to all the trouble and expense of getting everything in order and as you want it, only for the plan to go awry because you did not give it a few hours' attention maybe once a year. In fact, when there is any major change or upheaval, you should just give it the once-over and check with your Financial Planner that these changes will not make a difference.

Keeping abreast of changes to law and taxation, and economic circumstances, is essential. You want to make sure your plan factors in swings and roundabouts, and that you take advantage of any that will help you achieve it. How will you know whether any variations will affect you, and to what extent? Of course, this may be something you can do for yourself, but my experience tells me that most of you will want professionals to keep on top of these areas.

Undertaking these reviews, which will all raise similar questions, may come to seem a little repetitive. It will seem as if you are going through the preliminary steps all over again, and you would be right. You need to reassess whether your objectives, needs and requirements are the same as they were originally, adjust as necessary, bring everything up to date and satisfy yourself that you are where you want to be.

Professional help

By now you will have appointed a few professionals to deal with the different aspects of your Family Wealth Plan. It will be important that they work together on your behalf and not in competition with each other.

Look for people with professional designations, such as Certified Financial Planner (CFP™ professional). It will be easy to check out the professionals online. Recommendations can be valuable, but the friend or relative who referred them may have had different needs, so be sure the professional concerned can deal with your requirements.

Financial Planners can help you amass your information, analyse it, make sense of it and help you develop a strategy for your plan based on your goals and objectives. A good Financial Planner will get to know you and your family well, be able to work with them as a group or individually, sort out all the paperwork, appraise you of any necessary changes and carry out annual assessments of your circumstances, plans and investments. They will understand the detail of your plans and investments, and explain it all in plain English. They should make positive recommendations about what you should do and the steps to take once you have clarified what it is you want to achieve. This is the one person who should be able to liaise with the rest of your advisers and help bring all your requirements together. It means that everyone then works in your best interests, knowing that someone is overseeing it all. They can also act as a coach, mentor and overall project manager.

Some Financial Planners may work with wealth or investment managers on your behalf. If you use a stockbroker to buy and sell shares directly on your behalf (which a Financial Planner cannot do), they should still work together. The stockbroker needs to be clear about your investment requirements, your attitude to risk and how you will cope with any losses.

Is your portfolio set up for growth or to provide income? Are you an ethical investor and is impact or ESG (environmental, social and governance) investing now of interest to you? ESG criteria are a set of standards for a company's operations that socially conscious investors and managers use to screen potential investments and measure the sustainability and ethical impact of investment in a business or company. You will need advice from someone who is an expert in this area.

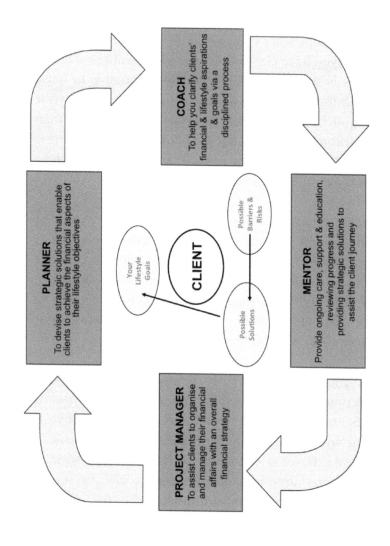

Roles of professional advisers

But back to your professionals: solicitors can specialise in many areas of work and you will definitely work with such specialists to draft your will, establish Powers of Attorney, set up trusts and carry out probate work. They will represent your legal interests and are usually experts in their chosen area of work. There are also estate practitioners who specialise in this work. Some Financial Planners work directly with lawyers and act as your liaison to save you having to visit one then another, but this is a matter of cost and convenience. Your Financial Planner will have all the information about you to hand that solicitors will need and save you time and effort. The solicitor will warn and advise you of any pitfalls in legal matters and bring these to the attention of your planner, so it is important that they work together. They will act on your behalf in any dispute, provide whatever legal documents you need and negotiate any legal agreements if required.

An accountant will be essential if you have any kind of business or property portfolio, or you are selling or transferring assets that have gained in value, and they often have expertise on taxation and can help you save unnecessary costs and make savings at the same time. The timing of some of your financial activities may be crucial, so involving accountants early could save you money. They ensure the financial health of a business, and Financial Planners task them with examining economic data and creating financial reports.

While solicitors, accountants and tax advisers may be the most obvious people to appoint, the list may include estate agents or surveyors if you own property and land. If health or care becomes an issue, then medical specialists and support workers may need to be consulted. Identifying those already connected with you and your family and linking up with some not already connected can help your overall planning.

Working together this way helps to maintain continuity and makes life easy for anyone having to deal with your estate after your death. When I was a probation officer, many moons ago, I worked as part of a multidisciplinary team that involved social workers, the police, the judiciary, solicitors, sometimes NSPCC and Dr Barnardo's, health workers and local youth leaders, even Citizens Advice Bureaux. At the time Alun Michael, who has been the South Wales Police and Crime Commissioner since 2012, was the Area Community Leader for one such area and worked tirelessly to bring all these groups together to help offenders and young people. The meetings held were invaluable in getting to know and understanding the community's cultures and how best we could work effectively using our respective expertise and knowledge for the improvement of people's lives.

A similar approach to engaging and communicating should be adopted among the professionals you employ for the eventual and successful implementation of your Family Wealth Plan. A collaborative approach gives you the most comprehensive service available.

Summary

Reviewing, reassessing and updating your Family Wealth Plan will become a regular habit and a good one. It will be one that will help you stay on track, feel in control and ensure you carry out your intentions.

Now you know what you need to know and which professionals you want on your side and supporting you. You will be clear about your decisions and why they are important.

EIGHT

H Is Forming Habits For Success

This is your life: live it well and get the most from it. End your days with few regrets. Think about how you wish to be remembered and what for. It is never too late to make amends to people you have hurt in the past or neglected. Sombre as all this may sound, people often end their days wishing they had done many things. Now is the time to make sure you are not one of them.

Making the most of your wealth

I imagine you have not accumulated your wealth without having received some advice along the way about investing it. It is surprising, though, how many people have not. Attorneys for relatives have presented me with a large range of savings and investments to look after. They feel an enormous sense of responsibility to do the right thing, and are overwhelmed by paperwork, which is why they seek my advice. The assets' owners have usually had to go into care, often with dementia, which means health and care issues that the attorney must give time and attention to.

CASE STUDY: SORTING OUT OTHER PEOPLE'S PAPERWORK

Dealing with the investments of someone who has received no advice can be a nightmare. You might unearth an array of savings accounts, shares with and without certificates, and will rarely find full details anywhere. They may have sold some of their investments, but you will not know until you try to contact the companies or managers. There may be land or property to deal with, value and sell: where are the deeds?

The attorneys for James and Emilia found three current accounts, five savings accounts and twenty-six other investments. We wrote to sixteen different companies for information on the holdings and had to send certified copies of the Powers of Attorney to each. Every page had to be certified. It was time-consuming but had to be done. Trying to put these investments in order and assess what the couple should keep or sell was step one. How much ready cash the attorneys would need for care costs and ongoing expenditure was step two. Analysing all the information and working out the tax positions, was step three. Step four was putting together the Family Wealth Plan the attorneys so badly needed.

Once each stage was implemented, finally it was a simple matter of regular reviews. The attorneys could access the couple's money, had funds to pay care fees, and we even carried out some IHT mitigation using BR investments (see Chapter Five). It was a toss-up whether to sell all the investments and accept taxable capital gains (some capital gains you do not have to count on death, so might have been better to leave invested). But since the attorneys needed regular *and* ad hoc access to the funds, it was important to provide for those; and some shares could be switched into ISA wrappers gradually.

Investing would be straightforward once the attorneys had established the level of risk they could bear and their capacity for any losses. A full and frank discussion finally determined this.

They ended up with two current accounts, two savings accounts and the rest merged, but properly diversified and professionally managed. They could complete tax returns more easily, reduce the paperwork and funds across the portfolio were more tax-efficient. This meant fewer sleepless nights for the attorneys, who could concentrate on the wellbeing of their charges, pay bills promptly and deal with any pressing requirements such as new spectacles or dental work for their relatives.

Putting together a strategy, including an investment element, was something they could not have managed alone.

To make the most of your wealth, it is not just a case of hiring a wealth manager, although that helps. You need to make your portfolio tax-efficient, to use the allowances available, possibly putting more into pensions (not necessarily for immediate tax relief but to mitigate IHT). As I pointed out in Chapter Two, pensions could be part of your planning for your family, even where you do not need them.

If married, are you making the most of each other's personal allowance? If you are both paying basic-rate income tax, up to 10% of one spouse's personal allowance you can transfer to the spouse paying more tax. Are you claiming relief on charitable donations or covenants? You can carry these forwards or back depending on your tax bill. If you receive rental income from properties, are you claiming the most you can for expenditure? Are you aware of what you now can and cannot claim? Although tax alone should not drive investment decisions, tax-efficiency improves returns.

Make use of any tax shelters, such as ISAs, check each year for capital gains and offset against the allowance. Consider whether tax saving investments are appropriate for you and your objectives. Since 2015, if a spouse or civil partner dies, ISAs in their name can be transferred to the survivor, without having to sell the investments and without affecting the current year's ISA allowance: it is known as the additional permitted subscription (APS). You must have been living with the deceased – if you are separated, APS is not available.

There are now many online investment platforms to choose from: you want one that you can access easily and understand. You can hold many investments on the right platform, including trusts, so keep everything in one place with a minimum of paperwork, which you can access and keep online.

You need to have some understanding of your investments and not just leave them entirely to your advisers. Find out how they manage the portfolio, since this can be crucial to capturing gains, even if small, and keeping you in line with your risk profile, so investment risk does not become greater than you can tolerate. In Chapter Five I discussed (for example) investments such as BR, which will mitigate IHT after two years of trading and can be cascaded to the next generation but are riskier; and in Chapter Seven ESG investing, if you wish to put your money into ethical or 'green' investments.

'Having some understanding' does not mean that you must constantly review your investments. In fact, it is best not to do this too often, since usually you will be investing for the longer term and short-term reverses should be expected and planned for. What do I mean? Short-term fluctuations are not real evidence as to how well your investments are doing. You need to view them over the longer term. Reviews should be a calm, annual routine, part of your Family Wealth Plan. It will make life easier for you, leaving you to enjoy your time, interests and family. It also makes it easier for others to pick up, if they need to step in.

Safe and secure

If you are going to enjoy the rest of your life without worrying about the security of your special possessions and documents, you also need to consider the less tangible assets you own and the intellectual property.

In today's world, you may not have got this far without having access to the internet, unless you have technology phobia. I have one client who does not own a phone, neither landline nor mobile, or a computer: we communicate by letter. No doubt you have several usernames and passwords to access your personal information, and electronic records of many kinds. Doubtless you also hold a ton of paperwork, personal (birth, marriage, divorce, health certificates), investment documents, important receipts and valuations, insurance policies, vehicle registrations, credit card records, passports, driving licences; the list goes on.

This means organising it all and keeping a system. Your family will thank you for organising it in due course, as will your attorneys, trustees and executors. If you are going to sort out your paperwork, make sure you use a shredder or burn the stuff you do not keep. Buy a fireproof safe that you can bolt to the floor, to keep precious items and important papers, and possibly also a small, fireproof and lockable filing cabinet for paperwork you want to keep at hand. This need not make your house look like an office, as quite attractive ones are available from furniture stores.

You will probably end up with a combination of hard-copy and electronic data, and a log of where everything is stored or saved will make the effort of preparation worthwhile. Remember to update your security software regularly to keep cyber-attacks at bay. These are growing increasingly sophisticated and need to be at the forefront of everyone's minds. Many people do not realise for some time after the event that they have been attacked.

To protect your data, it is best to keep your computer backed up, to keep a copy of everything. Back up regularly – you can set your computer to do it automatically. An external hard drive is quite inexpensive, simple to use and can provide an extra level of security, especially when protected with software that enables only you to access your data. Protect your devices with a password but make each one complex enough that they cannot be guessed or hacked, and be wary when working remotely. Some swear by password managers, such as 1password and Dashlane, but check them for yourself: there are plenty. Always log out of online accounts when you're finished.

There is a hilarious Michael McIntyre clip on YouTube about passwords, and there are some hard truths in what he says. As part of cybersecurity testing, my company plays our team this video first and then sets them a series of tests on protecting our information. Some of our clients have had their emails hacked, resulting in us receiving emails apparently from them, requesting to withdraw large amounts from their portfolios. For us, this is nothing unusual. The emails often look authentic; there may be nothing suspicious about them, but a request for bank details, or for money to be moved, always sets alarm bells ringing. A quick telephone call will reveal whether the request is genuine or not.

Most solicitors will store wills, LPA and trust documents for you for a small fee, but you should keep copies for reference. The OPG digital 'Use a Lasting Power of Attorney' tool will help those acting as an attorney to contact organisations like banks and healthcare providers more easily. Document storage companies, the Will Company for instance, can provide safe storage of valuable documents for a fee (these vary – some are annual, some daily) and often provide an identification card, carrying a unique reference. Retrieval is quick and easy with the card and identification documents with your photograph on them. Some banks will also store your valuables and paperwork by offering a safe deposit box, again for a fee.

Since 2013, deeds for property have been issued in digital form only, if you have registered the property with the Land Registry; you can get a scanned copy of these from the Registry should you not have the original. If you bought your property with a mortgage, the mortgagor often holds the deeds but you will need to check with the solicitor to see where they were sent or being held. If with the lender remember to get them returned when you have repaid your mortgage.

As you can see, there are many options for keeping data, paperwork and valuables secure. If you select one or a combination, inform your family and important people, so they know what to access and where should the time come. You have peace of mind and, with a little regular maintenance, can carry on with your life, safe in the knowledge that you have organised your affairs.

What if?

At the risk of repeating myself, your circumstances and those of others, your loved ones, friends and even your advisers may change. After all the effort you have put into arranging and rearranging your affairs, and putting them in order, a quite small event could throw some of them slightly off track. If you can prepare yourself for such eventualities and have some contingency plans in place, then hopefully there will not be too much upheaval.

Careful consideration needs to be made in setting up any LPA. If you have decided to appoint just two attorneys, to act jointly, and one of them dies, then the surviving attorney cannot act alone. In that case you can set up a new LPA and register it, but by that time, it is possible that you could have lost capacity. It might have been better to allow the attorneys to act jointly and severally, but another way to avoid this problem is to appoint a replacement attorney or two, to step in if specified circumstances arise. If you have lost capacity, there will be no other choice but for your family or the surviving attorney to apply to the Court of Protection for a deputyship order. This can be a long and expensive process, and if no one is able or willing to undertake the task, it will fall to representatives of your local authority to decide on your behalf how your affairs should be managed.

If you hold any life policies, in trust or not, the policy will usually name a class of beneficiaries as revocable or irrevocable. If you name a beneficiary as irrevocable, you cannot change your mind later, although the person named as the irrevocable beneficiary can agree in writing to no longer be the primary recipient. Conversely, if your beneficiary is revocable, then it is relatively easy to change a name on the plan. A Power of Attorney may give your attorney power to change the named beneficiary.

Let me now go through the impact of births, marriages, divorces or deaths. The birth of more children, say grandchildren or great-grandchildren, might prompt you to change your will, any trusts you may have set up and the amount of any specific bequests. You can include many generations in a will. (A family tree can be a useful object to keep with your personal papers so that any executors can easily learn who is who in your family.) You can easily and cheaply add a codicil (a supplement) to your will, and revising a letter of wishes is even simpler. Do not forget that people's names and addresses may change, even their gender, so keep these details up to date in your papers. Regularly revising a family tree may prove a good way of ensuring you include everyone in your will that you wish to.

A family member gets divorced and remarries? Think carefully before you alter your will or any trusts in these eventualities and what you would like to happen. If one of your beneficiaries dies before you, again, this is something you can try to consider beforehand and cover in any 'What if?' part of your Plan, although some trusts may not allow any changes – they may be 'absolute' or irrevocable once they are active. You can apply for a court order to change such a trust but there is no guarantee that the court will heed your wishes. Get into the habit of documenting everything, to avoid confusion and even disputes.

If you get divorced or remarry, then it is probably best to make a new will. On marriage any previous will is revoked, though divorce or dissolving a civil partnership does not invalidate it. However, many of its provisions might no longer be effective if you passed away before making a new will. For example, your former spouse or civil partner would be treated as having died on the date you completed your divorce or dissolution, so any bequest to them would fall back into the estate. If your will states that everything passes to your spouse (or civil partner), then it would be as if you died intestate (leaving no valid will). Moreover, if your will appointed your spouse (or civil partner) as an executor or trustee, divorce or dissolution would bar them from acting as such after your death. (This law does not apply in Scotland.)

Even where a child of a new relationship is yours, they do not automatically benefit from your wishes. Here, too, it would be best if you made a new will. Creating a trust after you have written your will, changing your mind about a beneficiary or making substantial changes could necessitate a new will. If you have responsibility for maintaining a child on divorce, it would be worth setting up a life policy in trust (or transferring an existing policy into trust) to cover maintenance costs. This could prevent claims on your estate by an ex-spouse and ensures that maintenance payments are maintained if you die.

However, changes of these kinds could probably be made in a codicil:

- Increasing the value of a cash gift, eg to reflect inflation

- Appointing a different executor, eg should the original executor die

- Appointing a different trustee, eg should the original trustee die

- Appointing a different guardian, eg should the original guardians divorce

- Reallocating a bequest, eg should the original beneficiary die

- Changing your funeral wishes, eg after buying a funeral plan

It is advisable to let your executor(s) know that you have added a codicil and tell them where you keep it.

Of course, the beneficiaries of your will can change it after your death, if they all agree to a deed of variation (also known as a deed of family arrangement). Such a deed varies a will (or the rules of intestacy) after your death. Beneficiaries may use this to redirect all or some of their inheritance to another person. There are many reasons why a deed of variation might be agreed to:

- To clear up ambiguities in the will

- To balance distribution between the beneficiaries

- To provide for someone omitted from the will, or

- To reduce IHT liability, say, by passing on to the next generation

A deed of variation can be executed before probate has been granted. Only beneficiaries who are over 18 years of age and have full mental capacity can agree to it. Once signed, the beneficiaries cannot change it.

If any of your advisers change, there can be continuity provided the firm or practice is still operating, and appoints someone to replace them; but this may not be true of sole practitioners.

Being forewarned and forearmed, with a bit of research and preparation before giving instructions, and talking through your wishes with your advisers, will help enormously. Moreover, even if none of these eventualities arise while you are still alive, they could cause enormous problems after your death, which I am sure you would wish to avoid.

Memories

For understandable reasons, in talking about cascading your wealth the emphasis is usually on money. It is all about the best ways of sharing your hard-earned assets with the people you care about the most.

However, I believe the most valuable presents you can give to them are some of your memories, the best ones obviously. Look around your home and you will find photograph albums, collections of music, art, literature, books, coins, watches, musical instruments. Some musical recordings may be your own, or there may be videos of you and possibly your family with friends at special events and celebrations. There may be heirlooms you want to pass on, but hopefully you will have itemised these in your will. Compiling a log of these memory capsules should be easy enough to do, but you need to make sure you are not passing on material that you have more interest in than the recipient.

Some memories are precious, personal, worthy of preservation and of interest to the next generation. Sharing them allows you to give a clearer picture of who you are, connect across the generations and further those values you hold dear. They should be meaningful; are you passing on valuable lessons you learned, friendly advice you received? What would you tell your younger self now about how to approach love, life, money and health?

The psychologist Erik Erikson said that reflecting on what we have passed on to the next generation is one of the greatest tasks of life before we die.[38] This process of reminiscence has great value not just for us but for those we love. With today's technology there are many ways you can save your memories digitally and if you think you cannot manage it, get one of the younger members of the family to help you. They will probably be keen to assist and can teach you a few things along the way.

On a simple level, think of yourself being invited to *Desert Island Discs*, that well-known radio programme. A presenter asks celebrities to pick eight pieces of music or other recordings they would take to a desert island and say why. In between they weave their life story, what sort of upbringing they had, the relationship with their parents and family, their partner and their career. They can take to this hypothetical island the Bible, the Complete Works of Shakespeare, and one other book. Then they can add a luxury item (although not something that will make life easy on a desert island such as a camping stove or fridge freezer).

My husband and I often discuss what we would take; our love of music is so wide-ranging, I know I would find it difficult to choose and, having been an avid reader all my life, choosing one book would be impossible. Still, we have fun talking about it, arguing about the talents and finesses of this composer or that musician or singer. You can be as creative as you like or keep this exercise simple. You can get an external hard drive on which to keep your photographs and recordings or save them to the Cloud. Writing a book or journal is another good approach: you can write longhand or word-process, or speak and record, whatever suits you, but keep your statements brief and to the point. Your family does not want to read or listen to incoherent ramblings.

I have kept a note of my favourite recordings, books, pictures and so in a leather-bound notebook given to me one Christmas. Whenever I remember or hear something I really like, it goes in the book. I share it with my family, and they remind me of other much-loved items. Then I recall why it brings back fond memories or why I liked it originally.

If you are familiar with social media, you can upload pictures into albums to keep them organised, share with friends and look at them whenever you wish. Sites like Tumblr and Google+ will let you upload images of pretty much any size, though Instagram and Facebook will scale down your photos if they are too large. A site called Notion can hold all your tasks, notes and documents. You can sync it across many devices. Digital technology changes rapidly, so it is best to do your homework on sites before using them. On social media, you can easily share your memories with friends, but keep them private and not for public viewing. On death, you may want to ask someone to take responsibility for looking after the pages. Facebook certainly allows this. You could even create your own website; there are many hosting companies, and many templates to choose from. On your own site you can write stories, upload photos and videos, to share easily with everyone, and do pretty much whatever you want.

There are also services that will write and print a memoir (or autobiography) for you. The appeal is turning a life well-lived into the story of your life, to settle down and tell your children, your grandchildren, perhaps even your great-grandchildren. Some offer better printing and binding options than others. Then there is YouTube, where you can post your own videos. These take little equipment: often a mobile phone will be good enough to record yourself, or perhaps someone in the family has the expertise to do this. Finally, there is the good old scrapbook which you can buy from any large stationers or online. Some have names like 'Family Memory Books', so there is not really much excuse for not getting your recollections down for posterity.

Doing this sooner rather than later is best but try not to overindulge in nostalgia and forget the reasons for undertaking the task. If all else fails, buy a nice wooden box that you can keep your keepsakes in. Whatever you do, do something. Be more than just a headstone or ashes in a jar. Let others remember you, what you enjoyed during your lifetime, what life gave you and how your life was lived well.

Summary

I will admit that mulling over your life and possessions is not a simple task. To have to think about sorting out paperwork now and how you will keep it safe until needed can be quite daunting. This is especially true if, like me, you do not have the time or inclination to keep on top of it. Set it down as one of your objectives and allot time to complete it. It is amazing how writing your goals on paper can drive you to act on them.

More important, though, is to share your thoughts and memories somewhere, somehow. Your family and friends will be grateful that you took the time to think about them. These will be gifts from your life that will be as precious as any of the wealth you pass to them.

Conclusion

As you can see, cascading your wealth is not merely about writing your will, although that is a vital part of it. There are many other aspects of your life that you need to contemplate before you can issue directions/ instructions about giving away your assets, whether in your lifetime or afterwards.

First, what you have and own and what it is worth. What are your goals, what do you want to achieve and what are the values you hold dear? How much do you need for your own and your family's security? How do you stand financially in the event of a death, needing care, divorce or remarriage?

Does the family's culture and religion impact on your decisions and do some members have special needs that you need to consider?

How prepared are you to hold family discussions about inheritance and learn from younger family members about their hopes and dreams? Would you like to help build character, not just savings accounts?

How fair do you want to be in dividing up your estate, and how concerned are you about how much IHT your beneficiaries will pay?

Many questions, I know, but only you can provide the answers, possibly with some help and support. Let the professionals and experts deal with the technicalities and documentation. Provided you have made it clear to them what your requirements are and what is important to you, they should all work in harmony for your benefit.

Your Family Wealth Plan is your primary reference point, a six-step process which will help determine where you are now and where you want to be, a clear picture of your assets with details and analysis. It will provide a logical strategy to set out clearly the direction you are heading in, how to get there and what is essential to your journey. The scorecard below can show you how far you have come and what more you need to act on to complete matters. The sooner you plan and strategise for your financial future, plus that of future generations, the more effectively your finances will work for you. Knowing you are able to contribute to grandchildren's housing deposits or accommodate the complexities of blended family arrangements alongside your own lifestyle aspirations and goals will bring peace of mind.

Next steps

Complete the Family Wealthy Plan Scorecard below to show you what you need to act on to complete matters. (Score 10 for Yes, 0 for No, and 5 for Partly.) My firm UNIQ Family Wealth has the qualifications and experience to assist you to develop your Family Wealth Plan. We have been helping and supporting our clients for many years, and we hope many more in the future. UNIQ specialises in working with families; runs workshops for executors, trustees and attorneys; and encourages younger family members to start their own financial planning. Some of these people will inherit your wealth. Like you, we want them to look after it and use it well.

If you want to build your own Family Wealth Plan, contact us on theteam@uniqfamilywealth.co.uk

Purchasers of this book can also contact me for a free copy of my first book, *Boomers: Redefining Retirement*, or a piggy bank to get young people started on their own financial journey.

Family Wealth Plan Scorecard

Questions				Score
Do you have a clear picture of what you have and own and whether it's enough to last you a lifetime?	Yes	No	Partly	
Do you have a vision for your financial future?	Yes	No	Partly	
Do you know if you will have enough money if you required care?	Yes	No	Partly	
Do you have plans to protect your family in the event of your death?	Yes	No	Partly	
Do you have the arrangements in place to successfully pass your wealth to the next generation?	Yes	No	Partly	
Do you know how much inheritance tax your beneficiaries would pay in the event of your death?	Yes	No	Partly	
Are you aware of the different exemptions and allowances that are available to mitigate tax?	Yes	No	Partly	
Do you have Powers of Attorney in place?	Yes	No	Partly	
Do you have a financial plan in place for yourself and for passing on wealth?	Yes	No	Partly	
Do your dependants know where to find all of the key information in the event of your death?	Yes	No	Partly	

Scoring 10 for Yes, 0 for No, 5 for Partly

Score 0-25: At present you are very unprepared. Read the book to find out what is required and the 6 steps to creating a Family Wealth Plan.

Score 26-50: You still have a long way to go. You need to start on the six steps to creating your Family Wealth Plan.

Score 51-75: Whilst you have some things in place, there are still several matters to attend to.

Score 76-100: Congratulations, you have most things in place but would still benefit from having your plan reviewed by a professional adviser to ensure that you will achieve your objectives and are on track. Complete the scorecard online or visit us at: https://familywealth.scoreapp.com

References

1. 'Should You Leave Your Money To Your Children Or Spend It Now?', Saga.co.uk, 18 January 2018, available at www.saga.co.uk/magazine/money/personal-finance/inheritance/inheritance-debate-to-leave-children-your-money-or-spend-it, accessed 22 July 2021.

2. Daniel Priestley, '2019 is Crucial For Entrepreneurs', Dent Global, 31 December 2018, http://www.keypersonofinfluence.com/2019-is-crucial-for-entrepreneurs, accessed 22 July 2021.

3. PruAdviser, 'Family Wealth Unlocked', ENM100025719 01/202, 2021. Available from www.pruadviser.co.uk/knowledge-literature/insights-hub/igp-hub/wealthunlocked/?adv sr=1&advtsr=2&q=Family-Wealth-Unlocked, accessed 21 July 2021.

4. M Outrim, *Boomers: Redefining Retirement* (2018, CreateSpace/UNIQ).

5. S Rach, 'Are advisers ready for the intergenerational wealth transfer', FT Adviser, 13 July 2021, www.ftadviser.com/ftadviser-focus/2021/07/13/are-advisers-ready-for-the-intergenerational-wealth-transfer, accessed 17 September 2021.

6. Research commissioned by Quilter and undertaken by YouGov plc, an independent research agency. All figures, unless otherwise stated, are from YouGov plc. The total sample size is 1,544 UK adults, comprising 529 baby boomers, 501 Generation Xers and 514 Millennials. The survey was carried out online between 7 and 8 July 2020.

7. Aegon, 'Baby Boomers Hotspots Report 2019', available at www.aegon.co.uk/content/dam/ukpaw/hidden/baby-boomer-report-2019.pdf, accessed 21 July 2021. Aegon projected West Somerset to have the highest number of baby boomers in the UK in 2019. Over one-third (33.39%) of the population were aged between 55 and 73 years, 11,513 people from a population of 34,476. The coastal region has an average life expectancy of 21.1 years from 65. South Lakeland (not in table above) has the highest average life expectancy out of the top ten baby boomer hotspots, with an average life expectancy of 21.1 at age 65 (NB: rounding means this figure appears similar to the Somerset, Southwest and Norfolk, East lines in the table).

8. Cameron Charters, 'Fancy a comfortable retirement? It'll cost you £26,000 a year', *The Times*, 3 June, 2021.

9. Kate Palmer, 'Does a £440k pension buy a happy retirement?' *The Times*, 13 June 2021.

10. The Retirement Living Standards, based on independent research by Loughborough University, have been developed to help us to picture what kind of lifestyle we could have in retirement. They were published by the Pensions and Lifetime Savings Association. For 2021 figures see www.retirementlivingstandards.org.uk/, accessed 21 July 2021.

11. UNIQ Family Wealth chart, created by Graham Cater-Pugh, Senior Paraplanner.

12. 'Transferring Ownership Of Land Or Property', Gov.uk, updated 8 March 2021, www.gov.uk/guidance/sdlt-transferring-ownership-of-land-or-property, accessed 23 July 2021.

13. Consumer research conducted by Consumer Intelligence among 1,019 individuals between 19 and 21 February 2021.

14. Source: HM Revenue & Customs, 'Inheritance Tax Statistics: Table 12.1 Analysis of Receipts', available at www.gov.uk/government/statistics/inheritance-tax-statistics-table-121-analysis-of-receipts, accessed 9 July 2021. The table shows the amounts of inheritance tax received in each year to 31 March, irrespective of when the charge to tax arose. It is split into three categories. 'Transfers taxable at death'

are cash receipts for tax on assets transferred at death and include tax levied on transfers made within the seven years before death. 'Transfers to discretionary trusts' are cash receipts for tax on the transfer of assets during lifetime, arising almost entirely on gifts to discretionary and other trusts, but occasionally including other immediately chargeable transfers. 'Charges on discretionary trusts' are cash receipts for charges on discretionary and other trusts. The receipts figures in the table are based on accounting information. 'Additional non-cash' shows the tax satisfied through transfers of works of art, heritage objects and land to public ownership under the Acceptance in Lieu scheme.

15. PruAdviser, 'Family Wealth Unlocked'.
16. For current NRB and RNRB, see www.gov.uk/inheritance-tax, accessed 23 July 2021.
17. Carehome.co.uk, 'Care home advice & nursing home advice', available at www.carehome.co.uk/Advice, accessed 22 July 2021.
18. www.liveincarehub.co.uk, accessed 13 April 2021.
19. https://ukcareguide.co.uk/widows-pensions-and-the-bereavement-allowance, accessed 22 July 2021.
20. The Lifetime Allowance was frozen in 2021 for the next five years.
21. Esteban Ortiz-Ospina and Max Roser, 'Marriages and divorces', OurWorldInData.org, 2020,

available at https://ourworldindata.org/
marriages-and-divorces, accessed 23 July 2021.

22. See www.gov.uk/convert-civil-partnership,
accessed 23 July 2021.

23. For the text of the Act, see www.legislation.gov.
uk/ukpga/1975/63, accessed 23 July 2021.

24. For current NRB and RNRB, see www.gov.uk/
inheritance-tax, accessed 23 July 2021.

25. Age UK, 'Briefing: health and care of older
people in England 2017', available at www.
ageuk.org.uk/globalassets/age-uk/documents/
reports-and-publications/reports-and-briefings/
care--support/the_health_and_care_of_older_
people_in_england_2017.pdf, accessed 26 July
2021.

26. Martin M Shenkman, 'Religion and estate
planning', Wealth Management (27 September
2016), available at www.wealthmanagement.
com/estate-planning/religion-and-estate-
planning, accessed 26 July 2021.

27. PRC Inheritance Law, which took effect on 1
October 1985.

28. Merrill, 'Defining the purpose, process and
perspective of family wealth', Merrill white
paper 2019, available at www.pbig.ml.com/
articles/how-do-families-make-effective-wealth-
decisions, accessed 10 March 2021.

29. 富不过三代 (fu bu guo san dai). Literally: wealth
does not pass three generations.

30. M Outrim, *Boomers: Redefining Retirement.*

31. www.theprobateservice.org/duties-of-an-executor, accessed 26 July 2021.

32. Charities Aid Foundation, www.cafonline.org

33. 'What Duties and Responsibilities Do Trustees Have?', PruAdviser, 1 February 2021, www.pruadviser.co.uk/knowledge-literature/knowledge-library/trustee-duties-responsibilities-the-facts, accessed 26 July 2021.

34. Office of the Public Guardian, PO Box 16185, Birmingham B2 2WH; email customerservices@publicguardian.gov.uk; tel. 0300 456 0300; see also www.gov.uk/government/organisations/office-of-the-public-guardian, accessed 27 July 2021.

35. This can arise for a range of rather sad reasons (illnesses, accidents, for example) and is a complex area.

36. 'Law Society Research – 7% of Respondents Made Or Updated Their Will During The First COVID-19 Lockdown', LawSociety.org.uk, 2 December 2020, www.lawsociety.org.uk/en/contact-or-visit-us/press-office/press-releases/law-society-research-respondents-made-or-updated-their-will-during-the-first-covid-19-lockdown, accessed 28 July 2021.

37. 'Marriages in England and Wales', ons.gov.uk, 2017, accessed 28 July 2021.

38. Sean Brotherton, 'Passing on family memories: Facilitator's guide', revised June 2015, PassingonFamilyMemoriesFacilitatorsGuide.pdf (ndsu.edu) accessed 15 March.

Acknowledgements

I would like to thank my clients and their families who have been the inspiration behind this book, and Rethink Press, in particular Lucy McCarraher and Joe Gregory, who have mentored me and others through this process; Lucy, especially, has motivated, cajoled and supported me to get to the end. Then there was Joe Laredo who coached me through the planning stages, and the Bookbuilder Facebook group where the members have been a regular source of support and encouragement while working on my book.

Other contributors who provided some great ideas and resources include Daniel Priestley, Steven Oddy, Matt Thomas, Sapna Pieroux and Sophie Jewry.

I am grateful to my beta readers who took the time to wade through my manuscript and provide me with some honest feedback to help me improve and reword. In no particular order, D Gareth Lewis, John Luff, Sir David Carter, Lee Robertson, Stephen Oliver, Matthew Marais, Julian Gilbert and Guy Tolhurst.

Thanks also to the UNIQ Family Wealth team without whom I could not deliver advice to our clients and ensure they keep on track.

Also, to my friends and family for their support, and my daughter Laura Janes of Uniquity who has overseen all the marketing and helped create the scorecard.

Special thanks to my husband Richard for his forbearance and the amount of time he had to spend on his own during lockdown, while I sat at my laptop.

The Author

Marlene Outrim has been a Financial Planner for some thirty years, and before that was a probation officer for thirteen years. She was President of the Institute of Financial Planning (IFP) in 2010–12 and set up UNIQ Family Wealth because she felt the time was right to help others put together their own Family Wealth Plans. She has many loyal clients, some of whom she has known for over twenty years. In her book, a client is for life, and their interests, their hopes and dreams come first.

Her first book, *Boomers: Redefining Retirement* (CreateSpace/UNIQ, 2018), examines the changing landscape of retirement in recent years. She is also a regular contributor to and commentator in the media and press, continuing to present at conferences, both nationally and internationally, particularly about 'cascading wealth'.

As well as her qualifications in financial services and financial planning, Marlene is also competent to take instructions for wills and Lasting Powers of Attorney. Sadly, she has also had to complete probate for some of her clients.

Marlene is the founder and owner of UNIQ Family Wealth, which helps families and individuals lead more fulfilling and financially secure lives by making the most of their assets. UNIQ helps them to cascade wealth seamlessly from generation to generation. Whatever life throws at them, UNIQ will be on hand to guide them with their own personal Family Wealth Plan.

🌐 https://uniqfamilywealth.co.uk

in https://uk.linkedin.com/in/marleneshalton

in UNIQ Family Wealth

🐦 UNIQfw

Lightning Source UK Ltd.
Milton Keynes UK
UKHW021527151221
395651UK00005B/276